EVRA-SUAREZ AND THE MADNESS THAT FOLLOWED

PAUL MCCALLAM

PAUL MCCALLAM BOOKS

Copyright © 2023 by Paul McCallam

All rights reserved.

No part of this book may be reproduced in any form or by any electronic or mechanical means, including information storage and retrieval systems, without written permission from the author, except for the use of brief quotations in a book review.

Cover By: Yuriy Yashmolkin

ISBN: 978-1-7397077-4-3

CONTENTS

Introduction   v

PART ONE
BACKGROUND
1. The Match   3
2. Charged   8
3. The Hearing   11

PART TWO
VERDICT & REACTION
4. Decision   21
5. T-shirts   26
6. "He Used Sudaca or Something."   32

PART THREE
LOSING THE PLOT
7. The Report   41
8. "There is no Smoking Gun in there."   45
9. There's More to the Report than Meets the Eye   59
10. "People Might Not Realise They Are Racist."   68

PART FOUR
HANDSHAKE
11. "Bang out of Order."   79
12. "Apologies Were Necessary."   85
13. "The Barbarians are at our Gates."   88
14. United Against Fascism   92

PART FIVE
THE REASONS WHY

15. Food Fights	99
16. Modern Racism	105
17. No Surrender to Patrice Evra	110
18. An Accident	117
19. Final Thoughts	121
Bibliography	125
Notes	129
About the Author	139
Also by Paul McCallam	141

INTRODUCTION

On Saturday 15 October 2011, Liverpool FC played Manchester United FC at Anfield. In the 58th minute of the game with the score at 0-0, Luis Suarez, the Liverpool striker, fouled Patrice Evra, the Manchester United captain and left-back. The referee, [Andre Marriner], awarded a free kick. Five minutes later, in the 63rd minute, Suarez won a corner for Liverpool. Evra's job was to mark Suarez at Liverpool corners. This corner was the first occasion that the players had come together since the foul.[1]

As [Liverpool captain], Steven Gerrard, was preparing to take the corner, Evra moved towards Suarez in the goal-mouth. They spoke animatedly to each other. The conversation continued as they walked along the goal-line until Dirk Kuyt, the Liverpool player, came between them. Suarez then ran towards the near post in anticipation of the corner, and Evra ran with him. The referee having blown his whistle for the corner to be taken, which it was, blew his whistle again to stop play. His attention had been drawn to the exchanges on the goal-line involving Evra and Suarez. He called both players over and spoke to them to tell them to calm down. As the players walked away from the referee, Suarez put his hand on the back of Evra's head. Evra pushed Suarez's arm away. The referee called them back and spoke to them again. The players walked away from the referee again, and the corner was taken.[2]

Over the following months, this 'corner' was to have massive ramifications which transcended football. Liverpool-born Ronnie Doforo had supported Liverpool for 45 years. Prior to the Evra-Suarez incident, he would not have heard a word said against the club. His opinion changed. Doforo observed:

"The word 'negro' doesn't offend me – Martin Luther King used it repeatedly in his 'I Have a Dream' speech, which is on display in my front room. But this word has no place in the game of football."[3]

He continued: "Suarez should not have called Patrice Evra 'negro' and there can be no getting away from this. We all know what he meant – he said it enough times. As soon as Suarez admitted what he had said, Liverpool should have fined him and made him apologise, sending out the message that the club does not stand for racial abuse of any kind, instead of waiting for the FA to make a decision."[4]

Another LFC fan also born in the city, Andy Heaton, saw it differently to Doforo. Heaton put forward arguments that defended the Uruguayan striker. Even after Suarez had been found guilty by an independent FA panel of racial abusing Evra, he still supported him and also lashed out rudely at people who backed the victim.

With the conflicting opinions of Doforo and Heaton in mind, let's now try to untangle what took place and why LFC fans thought it necessary to take sides on what became a debate on race.

PART ONE
BACKGROUND

ONE
THE MATCH

Liverpool and Manchester United are England's two biggest and most successful teams. With both clubs coming from the same region, England's north-west, the rivalry is intensified. Their unparalleled accomplishments mean they are supported in large numbers by fans from Land's End to John O'Groats, and Thailand to Texas. As a consequence of these factors, their fixtures can sometimes be the main highlight of the Premier League season, irrespective of their league positions.

When the clubs kicked-off at 12:45pm the hosts, Liverpool, were chasing Champions League qualification whilst their rival from down the East Lancs Road were pursuing the title. Liverpool had won their previous three home games against the Red Devils which was their best streak since a run of nine in a row between 1972 and 1979. The last five league matches between the sides had seen four penalties given. And in both meetings between the sides during the previous season, a hat-trick was scored by a member of the home team on the day – Dimitar Berbatov at Old Trafford and Dirk Kuyt at Anfield.[1]

Up to this point in the campaign, Luis Suarez was Liverpool's leading scorer with 4 goals. Manchester United's top scorer was Liverpool-born, Wayne Rooney, with 9. This was to be Kenny Dalglish's 250th league game in charge of Liverpool and he boasted the finest record of all – 150 wins compared to Bob Paisley's 144.[2]

During the game-after the 63rd minute corner incident-Steven Gerrard put the Reds ahead from a free-kick in the 68th minute. Nine minutes from time, Mexican substitute Javier Hernandez equalised with a close-range header. The match ended in a 1-1 draw. The result meant United were in second place in the league and Liverpool were 5th sandwiched between Newcastle United and Spurs.

AFTER THE FINAL whistle-while returning to the away dressing room-Patrice Evra is visibly agitated. His teammate, Ecuadorian Antonio Valencia, said he could see his colleague was troubled. He explained the Frenchman is not normally angry after games. Valencia stated:

"I cannot remember exactly the words Evra used but he said that Suarez had said that he wouldn't speak to him because he was black. I think the words Evra used were words similar to 'Negro, no hablas conmigo'."[3]

Evra's Portuguese teammate, Nani, recalled that he always sat close to Evra in the dressing room and at the end of the game when he came in, his captain was upset. Nani remarked:

"I cannot remember exactly what Evra said but he was complaining that Suarez had said something racist towards him. He said that Suarez had said that he wouldn't talk to him because he was black. When he said this in English I think he used the word 'n****r' but in Spanish/Portuguese he used the word 'negro' or 'preto', I cannot remember exactly which."[4]

With the Frenchman feeling anxious a couple of teammates advise him to speak to their manager Alex Ferguson. The Scot was speaking to goalkeeper, David De Gea, when Evra approached him. Evra told Ferguson:

"Boss, Suarez called me a n****r."[5]

Ferguson then goes to the referee's room with Evra. Ferguson tells Marriner that Evra has been called a 'n****r' by one of the Liverpool players. Referee, Marriner, asks Phil Dowd, the fourth official, to make notes of the exchange. Marriner assures the Manchester United pair that he will include the incident in his official report when he files it to the Football Association.[6]

Walls have ears.

At half-time and full-time on matchdays, Ray Haughan, Liverpool's team administration manager normally stands outside the home dressing room, which is immediately opposite the referee's room and next to the away dressing room. He does this in case anyone needs anything. While he was standing there after the end of the game, he saw Ferguson and Evra come out of the away dressing room and go into the referee's room. Haughan heard the Manchester United manager say:

"I want to make a complaint because Suarez has called him a n****r five times."[7]

Haughan informs Damien Comolli, Liverpool's Director of Football Strategy and manger Kenny Dalglish that Ferguson has alleged Suarez called Evra 'n****r' five times. Frenchman, Comolli, who speaks Spanish, talks to Suarez to find out his version of events. Suarez says nothing inappropriate has happened but admits using the term 'negro' in response to Evra saying: 'Don't touch me, South American'. Comolli relates Suarez's remarks to Dalglish before Phil Dowd arrives to ask Dalglish and Suarez to come to the referee's room.

Dalglish arrives to see Marriner and Dowd without Suarez. Marriner tells the Scot the substance of Evra's allegations and warns that a formal complaint has been made. A few minutes later, Comolli arrives in the referee's room and relates his conversation with Suarez. Dowd asks Comolli to spell 'Tu es negro' – 'You are black'. Comolli claims there has been a mistranslation and that Suarez did not use 'n*****s'.[8]

AFTER THE GAME, Evra is asked for an interview by Stephane Guy; a French journalist working for *Canal+*. Guy had noticed the defender was very distressed coming out of the changing room. Guy first questioned Evra off the record. According to the reporter, it was his duty as a journalist to ask his compatriot the same question again on the record even if he was not spontaneously in agreement to talk about it. He asked him:

"Is this the first time that this has happened to you on a professional field?"

The defender replied:

"First time that it has happened to me, first time that a player has said racist things to me like that. I am really concerned because he has no need for that, he is a good player and then this. He tried to make me lose it. It shows that it was really to make me lose it, but at the start, well, we will see. It still hurts."

He went on:

"If it's by the fans, I won't say it's fine, because it's still a shame, but when it's a player who is playing the same game as you, it's even harder to accept. Especially when I think that he has played with teammates who were my colour. So, at the start, well I won't go into a big debate about it, we are going to see the arbitrator, there will be an investigation, there is the video. You can even see clearly on his lips what he told me at least ten times. So, I'm calm from that point of view."[9]

The next day, Andre Marriner submitted to the FA an Extraordinary Incident Report Form in which he referred to the complaint that was made by Evra immediately after the match. The FA then took the decision to investigate Evra's complaint.[10]

Later that evening, Suarez posted the following on his *Facebook* page:

"I'm upset by the accusations of racism. I can only say that I have always respected and respect everybody. We are all the same. I go to the field with the maximum illusion of a little child who enjoys what he does, not to create conflicts."[11]

TWO
CHARGED

On Thursday 20 October Patrice Evra was interviewed by an FA official in Manchester. The same official then quizzed Luis Suarez on 2 November in Liverpool. The Uruguayan was accompanied by an interpreter from LFC and an independent professional interpreter was also present at the meeting.[1] On the same day Suarez was interviewed, the FA also questioned Kenny Dalglish, Damien Comolli, Ray Haughan and Dirk Kuyt. Between 4 and 7 November, the FA obtained signed witness statements from Patrice Evra, Andre Marriner, Phil Dowd, Alex Ferguson, and Evra's teammates Ryan Giggs, Antonio Valencia, Javier Hernandez, Nani and Anderson.[2]

Behind the scenes moves were afoot to find a more informal solution to the controversy. Gordon Taylor the head of the footballers' union was trying to organise a meeting between the two players through Liverpool's PFA representative Jamie Carragher. And although Patrice Evra later stated that he would have been amenable to such a move, nothing came of it.[3]

So, on 11 November the FA asked two experts,

Professor Peter Wade and Dr James Scorer, to prepare a written report on the linguistic and cultural interpretations of the words "negro" and "negros" in Rioplatense Spanish (the type of Spanish spoken by Suarez).

Both experts were affiliated with the Centre for Latin American and Caribbean Studies at the University of Manchester. Wade worked in the Department of Social Anthropology and is a specialist in race and ethnicity in Latin America, with particular emphasis on black populations, genetics and sexuality; he has also worked on the ties between Colombian national identity, popular music and race. He learnt his Spanish mainly in Colombia, had been a fluent speaker for nearly thirty years, and has experience of Spanish usage mainly in Colombia, Mexico and Spain.

Dr Scorer worked in the Department of Spanish, Portuguese and Latin American Studies. His research focused on Latin American cities, particularly urban politics and cultures in Buenos Aires, as well as on national and regional identities in Latin American cinema, including that of Uruguay. He learnt his Spanish predominantly in Buenos Aires and had been a fluent speaker of Castellano for nearly ten years.[4]

ON 15 NOVEMBER Professor Wade and Dr Scorer presented a written report to the FA. The next day, the forward was charged with misconduct contrary to FA Rule E3. The allegation stated Suarez used abusive and/or insulting words and/or behaviour towards Patrice Evra contrary to Rule E3(1), and that this breach of Rule E3(1) included a reference to Evra's ethnic origin and/or colour and/or race.

Suarez denied the accusation and requested a personal hearing. He told the Uruguayan media:

"There is no evidence I said anything racist to him. I said nothing of the sort. There were two parts of the discussion, one in Spanish, one in English. I did not insult him. It was just a way of expressing myself. I called him something his teammates at Manchester call him, and even they were surprised by his reaction."[5]

Liverpool Football Club also issued a statement. It read:

"The club this afternoon received notification from the Football Association of their decision to charge Luis Suarez and will take time to properly review the documentation which has been sent to us. We will discuss the matter fully with him when he returns from international duty, but he will plead not guilty to the charge and we expect him to request a personal hearing. Luis remains determined to clear his name of the allegation made against him by Patrice Evra. The club remain fully supportive of Luis in this matter."[6]

Liverpool boss Kenny Dalglish had previously asserted that he did not think that racism was prevalent at the club. He pronounced:

"I think the statement says everything and our position has not changed. That is all we've got to say."[7]

Piara Powar, executive director of the Football Against Racism in Europe (FARE) network, declared:

"Everyone knows from talking to ex-players that this is the sort of problem that went on. And now we see in 2011, going on 2012, it's still an issue. And we see the FA charging someone. I think that's right. Suarez, whatever his perspective on what was said or what wasn't said, and Evra should both have their day in court, so to speak, and bring any evidence to an FA tribunal."[8]

THREE
THE HEARING

The FA hearing got under way just after 3pm on Wednesday 14 December. The FA tribunal comprised of three men: Paul Goulding QC, a specialist in employment law who also held FA coaching qualifications; Brian Jones, the chairperson of Sheffield and Hallamshire FA; and Denis Smith, the former Stoke City centre-half and the ex-manager of York City, Sunderland and Oxford United. Despite being appointed by the FA, the members of the panel were independent from it.

The commission's job was to address the following:

"On the balance of probabilities, is the account of Mr Evra true and reliable?

If it is: (a) does that mean that Mr Suarez used abusive and/or insulting words and/or behaviour towards Mr Evra, in breach of Rule E3(1); and

(b) if it does, did the abusive and/or insulting words and/or behaviour of Mr Suarez include a reference to the ethnic origin and/or colour and/or race of Mr Evra within the meaning of Rule E3 (2).[1]

On the first day, referee Andre Marriner gave evidence,

then the hearing adjourned at 6:20pm. The next morning, Evra, Giggs, Suarez, Kuyt, Comolli and Dalglish all gave evidence. Evra and Suarez gave their testimonies on the same day; therefore, the FA panel could compare the evidence of one against the other, which helped in forming their view regarding the credibility and reliability of the evidence.

As we mentioned in the *Introduction*, (the FA hearing heard that) it was Evra's job to mark Suarez at corners. At the corner the Manchester United defender moved close to the Liverpool forward so that he could mark him. Evra faced up to Suarez and kept walking towards him. This forced the striker to move backwards along the goal-line and, in fact, slightly behind the goal-line. All the while, they were talking to each other. They reached a position approximately halfway along the goal-line when LFC's Netherlands' striker, Dirk Kuyt, stepped in between the two of them. The Dutch forward then prodded Evra in the chest. The Frenchman pushed Kuyt away with both hands against his chest. At this point, Suarez started a run out of the six-yard box towards the near post; Evra ran with him. The Uruguayan forward flicked the ball on into the goalmouth with his head, and then Marriner blew his whistle to stop play.

Both players agreed they spoke to each other in Spanish in the goalmouth. Evra noted that he was not exactly fluent in Spanish, but that he could easily converse in it. Evra alleged that he began his conversation with Suarez by saying: "Concha de tu hermana." According to the Evra, this is a phrase used in Spanish like "f*****g hell" in English, but the literal translation is "your sister's p***y". Suarez did not hear Evra say this. One of the video clips appeared to support Evra's evidence that he started the conversation with this comment.[2]

The Liverpool forward recalled he did not hear this first comment from Evra but that he heard him whispering something. Suarez informed the panel that he then said, "What did you say?" Evra told the hearing that he then said to Suarez "Porque me diste un golpe?" meaning "Why did you kick me?"

The French left-back stated that when he asked this question, he was in shock and upset at having been kicked in the knee by Suarez. The Uruguayan agreed that, at this point, Evra had asked him why he had kicked him, referring to the earlier foul in the 58th minute. That was largely the end of the agreement between them as to what was said in the goalmouth.

Evra's evidence was that, in reply to his question "Why did you kick me?", Suarez replied, "Porque tu eres negro."

The defender contended that at the time Suarez made that comment, he understood it to mean "Because you are a n****r." During the hearing, he mentioned that he now believed the words used by Suarez meant "Because you are black."

Suarez claimed he replied to Evra's question "Why did you kick me?" by saying "Que habia sido una falta normal", meaning "it was just a normal foul".

The Uruguayan added he then shrugged his shoulders and put his arms out in a gesture to say that there was nothing serious about it. Evra said that he followed up the striker's reply – "Because you are black" – by saying "Habla otra vez asi, te voy a dar una porrada", which means "Say it to me again, I'm going to punch you".

Suarez responded by saying, "No hablo con los negros."

The Frenchman remarked that, at the time, he thought

this meant "I don't speak to n*****s", although he later recognised it means "I don't speak to blacks".

Suarez claimed that Evra replied to the comment "It was just a normal foul" by saying "Okay, you kicked me, I'm going to kick you." Suarez said in his witness statement that his response was:

"Le dije que se callara e hice un gesto breve con mi mano izquierda parecido a la mocion de un 'pato cuando hace cuac' para indicarle que hablaba mucho y deberia callarse."

Which was translated as:

"I told him to shut up and made a brief gesture with my left hand like a 'quacking' motion as if to say he was talking too much and should be quiet."

The Manchester United captain asserted that after Suarez said, "I don't speak to blacks", he said, "Ahora te voy a dar realmente una porrada," which means "Okay, now I think I'm going to punch you."

To this, he says that Suarez replied:

"Dale, negro... negro... negro."

At the time, Evra believed this to mean "Okay, n****r, n****r, n****r". He now said it meant "Okay, blackie, blackie, blackie."

The expert witnesses stated that the phrase "dale, negro" could be understood as "bring it on, blackie" or "do it, blackie" or "go ahead, blackie".

Evra said that as Suarez was speaking, he reached out to touch Evra's arm, gesturing at his skin. Evra suggested that Suarez was drawing attention to the colour of his skin. This gesture is clearly shown on the video footage, just as Kuyt comes between them.[3]

IN CROSS-EXAMINATION, the United captain commented that at the time he did not realise that Suarez had pinched his arm. He was more focused on his lips and what he was saying. Evra only realised that the LFC forward had touched his arm in this way when he saw the video footage later.

Regarding the pinching of the full-back's arm, the striker proclaimed:

"Evra did not back off and Dirk Kuyt was approaching us to stand between us. At this point I touched PE's left arm in a pinching-type movement. This all happened very quickly. I was trying to defuse the situation and was trying to intimate to Evra that he was not untouchable by reference to his question about the foul. Under no circumstances was this action intended to be offensive and most certainly not racially offensive. It was not in any way a reference to the colour of PE's skin."

Suarez said that at no point did he use the word "negro" during the exchange with Evra in the goalmouth.

Evra claimed that up to that point, Suarez had used the word "negro" or "negros" five times in the goalmouth: "Because you are black," "I don't speak to blacks" and "Okay, blackie, blackie, blackie."

The referee then stopped the game. Marriner explained that he had been told on his headset by the assistant referee that there was a coming together between the two players and to get them over and tell them to cut it out.

Evra said that while he was walking towards the referee, he said, "Ref, ref, he just called me a f*****g black." He said that he did not know whether the referee heard his comment. The referee said something like "Calm down, Patrice, the game has been brilliant, stop the pushing between you and Suarez, the game is going well."[4]

Suarez claimed that simultaneously with the blowing of the whistle, Evra said to him:

"Don't touch me, South American."

The Uruguayan took this to be a reference to him touching Evra's arm on the goal-line a few moments earlier. Suarez claimed that he turned to the Frenchman and said:

"Por que, negro?"

He said that he used the word "negro" at this point in the way that he did when he was growing up in Uruguay, which was as a friendly form of address to people seen as black or brown-skinned or even just black-haired. He added he used it in the same way that he did when he spoke to Glen Johnson, the black Liverpool player. He alleged that in no way was the use of the word "negro" intended to be offensive or to be racially offensive. It was intended as an attempt at conciliation.

After Marriner had spoken to the two players, they walked away from the referee in the direction of the goal-mouth. They walked side by side. The Liverpool player stretched out his left arm and put his left hand on the back of Evra's head. The French left-back immediately and firmly pushed Suarez's arm away. The referee called them back and spoke to them again. He spoke first to Suarez and then briefly to Evra. United's captain made a comment as he and the Liverpool striker walked away, and Suarez can then be seen making a comment to Evra.

Evra's testimony of this incident was as follows:

"As he and Suarez walked away from the referee, Suarez put his hand on Evra's head. Evra pushed his hand away as he did not want Suarez to touch him. The referee must have seen this as he called them over and told them to calm down. The referee told Suarez not to touch Evra as Evra was saying he did not want Suarez to touch him. As they walked away Suarez said something to Evra, but he did not remember what he said to him or what Evra said to Suarez."[5]

Suarez's account was:

"The referee called the players to him the first time. Suarez did not understand what the referee was saying but he gained the impression that what he was doing was to say that they should each say sorry to each other and get on with the game. As they walked away from the referee, Suarez took his advice and patted Evra on the back of the head. According to Suarez, this was 'a friendly gesture designed to be conciliatory', but Evra reacted adversely to it and quite violently pushed his arm away. At that point, the referee called them both back again to him, spoke to them again and, Suarez believed, delivered the same message about getting on with the game. There was no more conversation between Evra and Suarez for the rest of the game."

It was at this point in his witness statement, having referred to these incidents, Suarez said:

"It seems to me that PE misunderstood my use of the word 'negro'. As I have said, it was meant in a conciliatory and friendly way in the context in which I have used the word throughout my life and as set out earlier in this statement."[6]

On Friday 16 December, a little after 3pm, closing submissions ended and the commission then began its deliberations.

PART TWO
VERDICT & REACTION

FOUR

DECISION

The commission reached its decision around 3pm on Tuesday 20 December and it was announced to the parties at approximately 6:20pm. The FA revealed the verdict publicly about 8pm. Suarez was found guilty of racially abusing Evra. He received an eight-match ban and a £40,000 fine; he was given fourteen days to appeal against the decision. The FA said the penalty was suspended until after the outcome of any appeal that might be requested by the Uruguay striker.

Liverpool responded defiantly. It was reported that they were set to appeal after being left shell-shocked by the guilty verdict. They accused the FA of deliberately setting out to punish their player even before hearing the evidence. The full statement read:

"We find it extraordinary that Luis can be found guilty on the word of Patrice Evra alone. No one else on the field of play – including Evra's own Manchester United team-mates and all the match officials – heard the alleged conversation between the two players in a crowded Kop goalmouth. It appears to us that the FA were determined to bring charges against Luis Suarez, even before interviewing him at the beginning of November. Nothing we have heard in the course of the hearing has changed our view that Luis Suarez is innocent of the charges brought against him and we will provide Luis with whatever support he now needs to clear his name. Evra admitted himself in his evidence to insulting Luis Suarez in Spanish in the most objectionable of terms. Luis, to his credit, actually told the FA he had not heard the insult."[1]

Liverpool also believed the Manchester United player of being "not credible". That was a reference to Evra's disciplinary case in 2008 when he was banned for four matches and fined £15,000 after an altercation with a Chelsea groundsman. The FA hearing at the time ruled his evidence was "exaggerated and unreliable" and Liverpool made a great point of focusing on this during the Suarez case.[2]

Suarez himself responded on *Twitter* by saying:

"Today is a very difficult and painful day for me and my family. Thanks for all the support."[3]

Kenny Dalglish, tweeted:

"This is the time when Luis Suarez needs our full support. Let's not let him walk alone."[4]

As we mentioned before, the club were contemplating an appeal, with the punishment suspended and Suarez free to play until the process was completed. The language of their statement made it clear they would not envisage taking their own disciplinary action.

PIARA POWAR, from FARE, had a different outlook to LFC. He remarked:

"This is a big moment and I would say that the FA have

dealt with this in the right way. They have taken their time and taken independent advice. No one takes any pleasure from seeing him found guilty like this, but it is an interesting judgement."

Powar added that FARE had taken advice on the abusive word used by Suarez and the context of similar words in South American dialects. He observed:

"If it is used in a friendly fashion then it is acceptable; it turns immediately to a hostile meaning if it is used as an offensive word. Taking the context of that game, it is difficult to see how he would have used it in a friendly way."[5]

The then Professional Footballers' Association chairman, Clarke Carlisle, believed the verdict was "100% correct". He told *BBC Radio 5 Live*:

"There are definitely cultural differences for a lot of players coming from South America and from the continent into England. But even though those differences do exist, we still expect people who come and work here to adhere to the standards and the laws of this land. It's wholly acceptable in parts of the Middle East to chop off the hands of thieves, but we wouldn't tolerate it here and it's just the same when it comes to racism."[6]

PFA chief executive Gordon Taylor commented:

"I was surprised at the severity of the punishment – bearing in mind the length of time the case took. That suggested there was some doubt about the claims. But it shows the FA must have some compelling evidence."

Taylor also believed clubs usually implement a 'them and us' attitude against the FA when their players are investigated by the FA. He claimed:

"They almost automatically support their players. But some things are bigger than clubs, players and even the game itself. Racism is one of them."[7]

THE UK MEDIA'S reaction to Suarez's ban and fine was mainly unsympathetic towards the Liverpool forward. Paul Joyce in the *Daily Express* wrote:

"The stain on his character is one he will struggle to shift. It is that stigma which will be more hurtful than the unprecedented eight-match ban he received. [...] Liverpool must now tread carefully. The continuing unequivocal support for Suarez comes without any apparent acceptance that he did not need to become involved with Evra. That he could simply have turned the other cheek."[8]

The *Daily Mirror*'s David Maddock stated:

"Questions must also be asked as to why the club was so swift to accept their player's explanation of events on that fateful October afternoon when Evra first made his allegations. There was no internal enquiry into the incident, and Dalglish will feel betrayed, as his own reputation is hauled over the coals, along with that of his club, because he had every right to expect the player to give him the full facts. He also had every right to expect more of Suarez."[9]

Ian Ladyman in the *Daily Mail* homed in on Dalglish's role:

"Liverpool's manager ought to be taking stock of exactly what it (the ban and fine) means ... He [Dalglish] now has a responsibility to Liverpool and indeed to football to ensure that Suarez understands the grave nature of the offence. As Liverpool manager he is right to stand by his player. He knows Suarez better than most. But Dalglish must also do what he can to ensure this never happens again."[10]

One of the few supportive voices from the press came from the *Liverpool Echo*'s James Pearce. He wrote:

"The fact is this was a case of one player's word against

another's. Remarkably, the three-man panel decided that Evra was the more reliable witness."

Pearce continued by discussing the nuances of South American languages:

"The word 'negro' is Spanish for black and in his native South America it is not deemed to be offensive. Someone with black hair is often called that without any malice intended."[11]

As we have just seen and contrary to Pearce's observations, FARE had had guidance on the word and its use in context. In addition, the FA Report would later state:

"First, there are some black people in Uruguay and other areas of Latin America who object to the use of the word 'negro' as a term of address, as they say it highlights skin colour when this should be irrelevant. This is the use of the word 'negro' (i.e., as a term of address) which Mr Suarez contended before us is acceptable, yet his view appears to be contentious with some in Uruguay and Latin America."[12]

With this mind, it would be interesting to know what expert advice Pearce was given before penning his article.

FIVE
T-SHIRTS

The evening after the decision, LFC played away at nearby Wigan Athletic. With the game being so local Liverpool travelled on the day of the game. When they arrived, they had lunch and then a team meeting. During the meeting one of the management team asked the players

"Are you still wearing the shirts?"[1]

The answer was clearly "yes" because during the warm-up before the game, the Liverpool players and manager Kenny Dalglish wore T-shirts in support of Suarez. The T-shirts featured Suarez's image on the front and his name and number on the back. During the post-match interview, Kenny Dalglish was asked:

"In the light of the events of the past 24 hours, was it a difficult decision to select Luis Suarez tonight?"[2]

The Liverpool boss replied mockingly:

"No, he wasn't injured."

The reporter then inquired:

"But his mind. Do you feel his mind was right?"

Dalglish replied:

"I don't think his mind is ever wrong, so we don't have a problem [...]."

Dalglish moves the conversation away from the matter being debated by discussing protection his forwards deserve from referees. The interviewer brings the focus back to the subject at hand. He asks:

"Sorry to ask one more question about Luis Suarez. The support from the supporters from the first whistle, and I noticed the players came out to warm up with a Luis Suarez shirt. It shows there's a major unity behind your player at the moment?"

The Reds' manager answered:

"So there should be. We've said, 'we'll always support him', and we will. And that's not just people at the football club, that's people who the football club means something to. And they know Luis Suarez means a great deal to them. He's got mutual respect for the fans."

Ominously, he warned:

"So, there's a fantastic relationship there and nothing will break it."[3]

LFC goalkeeper, Jose Reina, voiced the following:

"He has our full support. We were together from the very first minute of the allegations and [the T-shirts] were the minimum we can do for him. I am 100% he is not racist, and he has been accused of racism. We want him and everyone to know we are right behind our team-mate because he is a lovely guy, and he has been crucified by some people and it is not fair. Eight games is not even close to being fair."[4]

Former Reds player Howard Gayle saw things differently to Reina. Gayle, who is from the city and was the first black player to represent the club, thought it was poor judgement by the club to allow the players to don the T-shirts. In fact, it sickened him. With the Reds having worldwide appeal he believed some fans would no longer be following the club. He also noted that there would have been a lot of Liverpool fans who would have been offended. Furthermore, he expressed his disappointment in relation to the club who were thinking about challenging the ban.[5]

EVRA HIMSELF TUNED into the game. He found it mind-boggling. He was watching in disbelieve with his teammates and Alex Ferguson. The worst part for the Frenchman was this was after the ban had been put in place.[6] He remarked:

"[...] I was watching the game. I was like, this is ridiculous. It is unbelievable. Even for the club, you put your own club in danger when you do those things. I understand you always have to support your player because this is your team. But this was after the ban. If it was before the ban and you are waiting for the sanctions, but he got the ban. So what message are you sending out to the world when you do that? Supporting someone who has been banned for using racist words?"[7]

In October 2019, the ex-Liverpool player, Jamie Carragher, who played at Wigan, appeared on television alongside Evra. In relation to the T-shirts, Carragher accepted the club and players made an error of judgment. He stated:

"There is no doubt that we made a massive mistake. [...] I am not lying on that and saying 'I wasn't a part of it' because as a club, we got it wrong and we were all part of it. I was vice-captain. But that was the first I had heard of it that afternoon. So, I am not sure who was actually behind it."[8]

On Dalglish he went on:

"[...] I don't think Kenny had anything to do with it, to be honest, it was the players who Luis was close to in the dressing room who really wanted to support their mate and their friend."

On his own behaviour, he contended:

"What I would say is that maybe I, as an individual, lacked the courage to say I wasn't wearing it. Because once the squad has decided [...] I have to look at myself. I didn't have enough courage. Maybe there were others. I don't think everybody within Liverpool thought that we were doing what was right. But as a family, as a football club, your first reaction - no matter what someone does - is to support them even if they are wrong. And that is wrong. I am not condoning it, but that is the first reaction. Apologies. We got it massively wrong."[9]

Magnanimously, Evra responded:

"Actually, I understand. The first reaction of your club and your teammate is to support you. If I made a massive mistake and I see my teammates or the club doesn't support me, I would feel they were letting me down. So, I understand, and I don't understand. It is 50-50."[10]

After Carragher and Evra's appearance on TV in 2019, LFC finally apologised properly to him. He received a letter from the club saying he was welcome at Anfield at any time.[11]

THE DAY after the Wigan game, Paul McGrath, the former Manchester United, Aston Villa and Ireland defender, called Liverpool's decision to wear the T-shirts "shameful". McGrath expressed this opinion:

"Maybe Kenny [Dalglish] is trying to make a statement to the FA but I just think it is in bad taste that he sent them out in those T-shirts. It would have been much better for Liverpool Football Club if they had have worn anti-racism shirts. It's about respect [...]. There are a lot of children that watch these games and to have done what they did last night doing their warm-up in T-shirts with his smiling face on it, having just been done for a supposedly racist comment to one of his opponents, is shameful for football. It puts the anti-racism campaign back to the beginning as far as I'm concerned."

McGrath went on: "If I was in Glen Johnson's [Suarez's black teammate] situation, I'd have thrown the shirt to the floor. If that had been someone in my time and I'd heard the comments or I'd even suspected he was guilty – and obviously there has been a tribunal – then I would not wear a T-shirt with his name on it, saying all is well and good here."[12]

The Blackburn Rovers striker Jason Roberts tweeted:

"The stance on the Suarez issue from LFC has bemused me – are United going to print Evra shirts now????? Some issues are bigger than football."[13]

The former Newcastle United defender Olivier Bernard, who became an anti-racism campaigner, commented:

"I really didn't think it was fine to wear the T-shirts. I can understand the club's side of it, but in society we can't accept racism and give support to a player who has used racist words."[14]

Black Liverpool fan, Phil Boyle said:

"I also felt let down when the team warmed up in Suarez T-shirts. It was as if they were saying just because someone has racially abused another player doesn't make them a racist, which was irresponsible."[15]

Liverpool manager Kenny Dalglish doubled down in his support for his player despite the public outcry. He maintained the club's support of Luis Suarez had been 'right and proper' and had not 'caused trouble'. He defended the club's stance by insisting:

"The statement couldn't have caused anyone any trouble and I don't think the players have caused any trouble with the FA either by their statement or support by their T-shirts."[16]

Dalglish said Suarez had been moved by the show of support from the club and his team-mates. The Scot declared:

"He's been quite emotional and very grateful. I don't think it is ever a disappointment when the people you work for give you their undivided support and I think that is the least he deserves."[17]

SIX
"HE USED SUDACA OR SOMETHING."

On the day when ex-pros were condemning the conduct of LFC, an LFC fansite called the *Anfield Wrap* produced a podcast. The title of the broadcast didn't leave too much to the imagination. It was called:

"Suarez Reaction: The lads discuss the absolute fucking abomination of a case against Luis Suarez and the witch-hunt by the FA and certain 'members' of Her Majesty's Press".

The cast of the show included; (the host) Neil Atkinson, Jim Boardman, Giulio Canetti, Steve Graves, Andy Heaton, Mike Girling, Rob Gutmann, John Gibbons, and Steve Martin.

Atkinson opened the floor firstly to Andy Heaton. Heaton (who we came across in the *Introduction*) advanced this:

"A bit ridiculous really, isn't it, given they've banned him despite, if you believe the statement coming from Liverpool, that he's not a racist, so on what grounds have they actually banned him for [...]?"[1]

Next, John Gibbons criticises the FA panel, saying their decision was based on "Guesswork."

On the subject of racism, Heaton contends:

"You either are, or you're not."

Mike Girling suggests that Suarez is just "an unfortunate pawn in a game the FA are playing [...] and Suarez is just f*****g unlucky."

Steve Martin tried to bring some fairness to proceedings by saying:

"[...] I know we're all kind of saying this is wrong, but just a bit of devil's advocate. Did Suarez use racist language during that game? He used the word apparently 'negreto', which apparently is open to interpretation as to the inclination of that word, but if he said it in a football match to another footballer player, can't we say he intended it to cause offence? Are we all saying that Suarez used that word in a friendly like way?"

After Martin's coherent statement, uproar of sorts ensues. Atkinson tries to bring order to proceedings:

"Woah – one at a time". He gives the floor to Heaton. Heaton responds with:

"Right, if you believe what's been said, right, whatever Suarez said to Evra has followed an insult from Evra to Suarez, he used the word 'sudaca' or something."

For the record, at no point did Evra use the word 'sudaca'. The word "sudaca" was referenced in the FA report. The report stated:

"Mr Suarez told us that he said 'Por que, negro?' in response to Mr Evra saying 'Don't touch me, South American.' At one point in his interview with the FA, Mr Suarez said that Mr Evra used the words 'Don't touch me, sudamericano'. In his evidence to us, he said that Mr Evra's words were 'Don't touch me, South American,' all in English."²

The report continued:

"The Spanish language experts said that they were not familiar with either 'sudamericano' or 'South American' being used as an insult, although if used with a sneer it might well be understood as such. A more derogatory insult along these lines would be the term 'sudaca', a term most frequently used in Spain to label South American immigrants."³

As we can see, the word "sudaca" is not coming from Evra's lips, it is coming from the experts, and it is being used in a hypothetical sense.

Heaton proceeded with:

"Now, we were talking about this last night, it's one of them. It's a playground spat, you know, I'm not excuse... [his voice trails off].

If it hadn't already his defence of Suarez then enters the realms of the peculiar:

"If he's used the word 'negreto', he's used the word 'negreto.' There's two things here, if the word 'negreto' wasn't actually the word 'negreto' and began with a different letter, I don't think ... [his voice becomes inaudible]."

Heaton then suggests:

"Secondly, we've all done it. Not used racist language. But you see it all the time in playground spats, someone calls you a 'fat b*****d'."

The host interrupts his friend: "So, what did Evra say to Suarez, Andy?"

Heaton informs the other panellists:

"He allegedly called Luis Suarez 'sudaca', which, according to Wikipedia, is a Spanish colloquial term used most typically in Spain to denote people from Latin America in a derogatory manner or pejorative way. Now how is that different from..."

Atkinson then turns to Giulio Canetti:

"What's really interesting about this is if he's used that word [he didn't], this is a conversation that's taken place in Spanish, Giulio?"

Canetti's 'reasoning' was this:

"Well, it just says to me Suarez is probably not guilty, and in my opinion, not at all. Evra is definitely guilty [...], so these are facts, everything else is completely subjective."

Rob Gutmann puzzlingly asserts:

"[...] What I'm going to say is this. There needs to be a wider public debate about how a word that actually references skin colour or background actually doesn't have to be done in a derogatory way, even in the middle of a heated argument."

Next, Mike Girling, doesn't hold back in his appreciation of Daglish's backing of Suarez:

"The club's reaction, to be honest, tells me all I need to know. If you're going to line up against one of these entities, whether it's the FA or Evra, the club or Kenny, it's f*****g Kenny all day long."

Next, Atkinson runs with Girling's defence of "It's f*****g Kenny all day long". He maintains the vibe in the room by proposing this:

"Isn't the massive issue with this Mike? This is why I want to discuss – the vacuum the FA are leaving by not issuing any further information until the end of January. Therefore, we don't know, it's not even a matter of us having a balance of probability. We've got Kenny Dalglish, who is Kenny Dalglish by the way, turning around and saying as far as he's concerned, he's got 100% support for

Luis Suarez and he's Kenny Dalglish and I'll say it again he's..."[4]

THE PANEL then moves onto clearing Suarez's name. One panellists believes:

"This could be months, years, Court of Arbitration for Sport territory. I think ultimately the last precedent set found for the defendant."

Atkinson then goes on a rant about the *Daily Mirror* calling them despicable and he calls the FA despicable too for putting "us in this situation."[5] He then hands the floor again to Heaton. Heaton goes on about the Crown Prosecution Service and people calling him paranoid. He mentions the word "riddle" and then says that Rob Gutmann can explain his opinions more eloquently than he can. Unfortunately, Gutmann couldn't, so the riddles persist. Atkinson then speaks in further riddles about the incident basically being an "employment dispute". He then presents Suarez as the victim because of his potential "loss of earnings".

After more 'legal' discussion, Steve Martin offers this:

"That's the sad thing about this, isn't it? In a sense, Suarez was honest and said that 'I used that word'. If he'd denied using it, where would that have left us?"

Gutmann agrees:

"You're right [Steve], it's a good point. End of."

A worked-up Mike Girling says of the independent panel:

"That three-man panel is a kangaroo court, that three-man was irrelevant, that was irrelevant what that three-man panel said."

Martin then adds:

"I think they panicked once he admitted saying that word. I think that was his biggest let-down, is him being honest. I think he left them with very little choice."

Neil Atkinson then takes issue with the Kick-in-Out Campaign and Clark Carlisle from the PFA by suggesting they influenced the ban. He covers his tracks by saying that it might just be paranoia. Andy Heaton had no such qualms. He expressed this:

"Don't you think it was disappointing that they couldn't wait to get their own statement out even before the facts have been released by the FA before the appeal?"

Rob Gutmann then goes on a rant, which finishes with this really jumbled thought:

"[...] It's ridiculous. Let's just pick a guy up off the street and put him in jail for racism. Regardless of what he's done."

Possibly because of the tone in the room, one of them claims:

"Liverpool could sue the FA for defamation as far as I'm concerned. I think Suarez can sue Evra for defamation. They can take this way out of the FA's hands by taking it down the criminal court route."

The psychosis spreads to Canetti:

"The FA have declared war on us, as far as I'm concerned, simple as that, we've got no choice now."

Not to be left out, Heaton came out with:

"I think we've declared war on them to be honest."

Several of the panel then agree how proud they are of the "backbone" the club are showing in going against the FA's racism accusation against Suarez. Andy Heaton proclaims:

"I think they deserve a lot of credit for having the balls."[6]

THE PANELLISTS then move on to the T-shirt wearing. Steve Martin now moves away from playing devil's advocate:

"I thought it was brilliant to be honest. I thought it was great to show solidarity behind him."

He continues: "In a sense, not necessarily about what's gone on about the court case, but him as a person. To support him as an individual in a sense to try and remove this Sword of Damocles that's now over him and his family [...]."[7]

Atkinson then sums up:

"To sum this up, we'll discuss the Wigan game in the next proper podcast."

The summing-up was only temporary unfortunately, for Atkinson come out with:

"Giulio, you're saying this is essentially now a declaration of war and there's no way back for Liverpool and we should take it as far as humanly possible?"

Canetti's only concern seems to be that he might not see a LFC player due to the inconvenience of an 8-game ban. Atkinson then returns to Andy Heaton's monumentally bizarre theory of taking away the first letter of a word. He states:

"It's the first syllable of 'negreto' that's done massive damage."

And so, the madness begins.

PART THREE
LOSING THE PLOT

SEVEN
THE REPORT

On New Year's Eve, the FA released the contents of their findings in a 115-page report. In relation to the incident in the penalty area, the report stated:

"The whole tenor of the players' exchanges during this episode was one of animosity. They behaved in a confrontational and argumentative way. This continued at all times during their exchanges in the penalty area. Whilst Mr Evra is partly to blame for starting the confrontation at that moment, Mr Suarez's attitude and actions were the very antithesis of the conciliation and friendliness that he would have us believe."[1]

On the matter of Suarez using the word "negro" in a "conciliatory and friendly way", it declared:

"Once more, we were troubled by the fact that Mr Suarez advanced this case to us and relied on it to the extent that he did, when it was unsustainable. The suggestion that he behaved towards Mr Evra at this time in a conciliatory and friendly way or intended to do so in using the word 'negro', is, in our judgment, simply not credible. His evidence is again inconsistent with the video footage. Once again, there was no satisfactory explanation for this inconsistency."

Additionally, on the word "negro", it noted:

"Mr Suarez's account of his admitted use of the word 'negro' changed several times. He seemed unsure of when the admitted use took place and what triggered it. His account seemed to change in an attempt to fit in with the video evidence."

Even Liverpool's lawyer had doubts about some of Suarez's evidence. The report observed:

"Not only did we reject this evidence of Mr Suarez, but we found it remarkable that he sought to advance a case that was so clearly inconsistent with any sensible appreciation of what happened. Even Mr McCormick [his lawyer] accepted in his closing submissions that the pinching could not reasonably be described as an attempt to defuse the situation. To suggest otherwise, as Mr Suarez did, was unarguable. Mr Suarez's evidence on these topics, which was shown to be flawed, profoundly undermined our confidence in the reliability of his evidence."

The report continued:

"The impression created by these inconsistencies was that Mr Suarez's evidence was not, on the whole, reliable. He had put forward an interpretation of events which was inconsistent with the contemporaneous video evidence. He had changed his account in a number of important respects without satisfactory explanation. As a result, we were hesitant about accepting Mr Suarez's account of events where it was disputed by other credible witnesses unless there was solid evidence to support it."

Of Evra, the report commented:

"In contrast, Mr Evra's evidence was not shown to be

inconsistent with the facts established by other evidence, such as the video footage, in any material respect."[2]

Earlier we quoted John Gibbons who called the findings "Guesswork". Contrary to Gibbons' judgement, when the report was published, it emphasised the relevant evidence they were able to consider in reaching their decision. This evidence included video footage of the match; the evidence of others as to what happened during or immediately after the match; documentation in the form of the referee's report, which was based on conversations he had immediately after the match; transcripts of interviews with the main protagonists and other witnesses conducted in the course of the FA's investigation before witness statements were prepared for the purpose of the hearing; and the evidence given to them by other witnesses quite apart from Evra and Suarez, including expert witnesses on the Spanish language.

IN THE WAKE of the report Liverpool were considering their options. They had until January 13 to decide whether to appeal against the punishment. In a holding statement the club said:

"The club can confirm that they received the written reasons from the regulatory commission at short notice on the evening of the game against Newcastle United. The player, the club and our legal advisors will now take the necessary amount of time to read, digest and properly consider the contents of the 115-page judgment and will make no further comment at present."[3]

It was suggested in the press, given Liverpool's angry response to the verdict in December when they reaffirmed their belief that Suarez was innocent, that they would certainly appeal. However, it was also noted that they would be wary of the fact that could lead to an increased ban with the report revealing that the panel even considered giving the Uruguayan a "greater suspension".[4] However, it was also reported that the Reds' top scorer was expected to return to the side for the trip to league leaders Manchester City the following evening.

Piara Powar, from FARE urged Liverpool to abandon any thought of appealing against ban. He stated:

"The Football Association's published judgment from the Suarez-Evra incident is welcome. It appears the FA have taken their time to initiate a process that was both fair in its implementation of football rules and in accordance with the principles of British justice."

Powar continued:

"As an international non-governmental organisation we think the investigation and judgment sets the bar for governing bodies globally. Racial abuse between players on the field of play has been an unspoken taboo for too long, an area that has been unsatisfactorily dealt with by English football despite many cases over the past 10 years. Luis Suarez and Liverpool FC have the right to appeal, however we would call on the club to think again about their public campaign to dispute the charges and contest the principles involved in the case. As a club with a good international standing the vehemence of their campaign is unquestionably causing them reputational harm."[5]

EIGHT

"THERE IS NO SMOKING GUN IN THERE."

As we will see soon Luis Suarez, the club and his teammates reacted on 3 January. On 2 January the *Anfield Wrap* responded. When they brought out their podcast post-Wigan in December, the findings of the report were yet to be released. So, we could give them the benefit of the doubt and that's despite the absurdity of the remarks they put forward.

Once the information was published, it is very hard to comprehend how any rational British person in the modern age could defend Suarez. Therefore, it is important to keep this in mind when observing the views of the participants during this next show. It is also worth noting here that at the beginning of this broadcast, the host, Neil Atkinson, informs the audience that everyone in the room had read the report. So, there were really no excuses. Staying with the host, he begins by warning the audience:

"[...] If you don't like explicit or racial language being used, then I would recommend that you either spool for thirty minutes into the podcast or don't listen to it at all. If you're in the vicinity of children and you don't want them to hear these sort of words, please feel free to have a listen later. As I say, we're not going to shy away from the language."[1]

Atkinson's definitely correct about not allowing kids to listen to it, but not for the reasons he supposes. For the record, the panel is; Jim Boardman, John Gibbons, Mike Girling, Steve Graves, Andy Heaton, Jay McKenna, Steve Martin, Gareth Roberts, Rob Gutmann and Kristian Walsh. Atkinson's first question is directed to Jim Boardman and its wording tells us all we need to know about where the discussion is heading:

"Jim, what did you actually make of the way in which the evidence was stacked against Suarez?"

For many Anfield Wrap subscribers, Jim doesn't disappoint:

"[...] It read like a story to me, so you start at the beginning, and work your way through to the end. And to me it seemed like they were using ways to discredit Suarez that didn't get applied equally to ways that could have been used to maybe discredit Evra. So, well before I got to the point of the summary, I was already thinking 'there's things in here that don't add up, they don't match up'. To be honest it felt like all the way through that it was a forgone conclusion, like they were trying to make things fit into a preconceived answer."

Next up is Mike Girling. If you remember in the previous podcast, he went with the zealot's conviction of "It's Kenny all f*****g day long". This time he'd changed tact and took on the persona of Gregory Peck playing a lawyer in a 1960s blockbuster merged with a Harvard academic. In a remarkably different tone of voice than previously, he proclaims:

"There's a term for that Jim, it's called 'confirmation bias'. What that means is that 'what you've got is justification for a verdict rather than a body of evidence which talks about this is exactly what happened'. And the whole thing reads like that."

He proceeds with:

"But what bothered me more than anything is that if you read through the first 110 pages, the actual summary doesn't necessarily relate to the evidence that was in those 110 pages. The summary has got a lot of what a lawyer would call 'misrepresentations' in terms of fact, these are facts in the summary and there's no justification of that in the body for a lot of them, things like, 'he said negro 7 times', there's never ever any corroborating evidence to say that Suarez did say that. I think Suarez only admitted saying it once. Yes, so, a fait accompli and confirmation bias."

Rob Gutmann is up next, and you won't be astonished to know that he agrees with Jim Boardman that the report is basically a story that keeps labouring the same points. Jay McKenna then defends Suarez by claiming he didn't understand the questions properly because they were in English. This is despite the claim that the panel had read the document and Atkinson literally informs McKenna that Suarez had received the questions in Spanish. McKenna doesn't allow facts to get in his way. His justification was this:

"You watch press conferences with Andre Villas-Boas now [then Chelsea coach], you watch Benitez when he was manager [of Liverpool] they get asked a question in an interview and they just don't seem to understand it. And they give a half-hearted answer, and you sit there thinking 'what on earth I've you just said there because it's not what you've just been asked.' He [Suarez] doesn't understand it and they

[FA] then use that and say, 'it might be because he's got a poor grasp of English, but we believe he's inconsistent.'"

Unsurprisingly and despite McKenna's viewpoint being a fabrication, Rob Gutmann says:

"I agree."

Gutmann also attempts to explain the nuances of the language which occurred during the passage of play when Suarez pinched Evra. Gutmann believes that despite being involved in a heated confrontation, Suarez could have pinched Evra and been conciliatory towards him at the same time. He suggests any person can be angry and conciliatory at the same time and if so, they could use language such as:

"What's your problem, pal? Or 'Calm down, love.'"

Despite his examples above Gutmann then blasts the FA for its lack of a grasp of the subtleties of language. McKenna's next and he just rambles:

"Because they decided, well they've contradicted themselves for me. They've decided that it was going to be subjective, that it should be objective that he said this word. So, if you say objectively, he said the word [his voice tails off]."

Steve Graves is up next, and he believes the report was basically pointless. Gutmann insists that the report is so biased that it's bordering on racist. Andy Heaton then backs Suarez to the hilt:

"It was a 115-page character assassination, that's all it was."

Mike Girling believes:

"If you look at the contents of the report, you could easily have a verdict that exonerates Suarez."

And although Suarez admitted using a derogatory racist word during an altercation, he carries on by saying:

"There is no smoking gun in there. Anywhere."[2]

GARETH ROBERTS, thankfully, sees matters differently to many of his fellow guests:

"I think Liverpool's handling of the whole thing has been highly questionable to be honest. I think from a PR perspective the statements that they put out, the decision to wear the T-shirts, so on and so forth, ill-advised, when your reputation's on the line. For a club, we're talking about an incident with a player here. The club's bigger than the player, it always has been."[3]

Roberts next goes onto blame LFC's legal team for messing up the case. Andy Heaton then gives some background to the changes that have taken place recently in the club's legal set up and how the previous advisors would have handled the situation a lot better. To quote Heaton:

"It was a mistake by the club to go so balls out."

He goes onto state that he doesn't want Liverpool to retreat now because it would be a sign of weakness and show that they're willing to be dictated to by the media who:

"Haven't got a f*****g clue about what's gone on and have dived in, just condemn without reading the facts."

Heaton then takes the Girling and Atkinson (Dalglish) route from the earlier podcast:

"I trust Kenny Dalglish right. Put all the legal notes to one side. I trust and I believe in that man. And if he's backing Luis Suarez, fine, I'm standing by him. I'll stand by him more than I'll stand by anyone else at the club. If there's internal pressure within the club to pull back, I don't care, I'm going with what Kenny thinks on it."

Jay McKenna is not so sure of blindly following Dalglish, he also claims that going forward LFC should stand united. He criticises some of the club's behaviour, but then he asserts that it was a good move for the players to wear T-shirts in defence of the Uruguayan. He proclaims:

"I think it was good that players were united. We don't know what the players have decided, we don't know how they have come to the decision to wear them T-shirts. Whose idea it was, what discussions took place, they've made a decision and decided they should do it."

He then stresses again that LFC need to be careful and should not just stand behind Dalglish because he is Dalglish.

Like Atkinson, Rob Gutmann points out that the report is loaded against them. His next contention seems muddled from a 21st century British person's perception or just plain muddled because he doesn't know where to go with his argument. He notes they need to be steadfast behind justice, i.e., defending Suarez, but at the same time being sensitive towards people who fight against racism. Gutmann notes that fighting against racism is a noble cause, and he doesn't want to patronise these people. He recognises that he and his colleagues are unfortunately on the other side of the line against people who, in his words:

"Do some good stuff."

He continues: "And it's a difficult balancing act for us to go forward in our defence of our man and keep sensitive to that."

After McKenna's enthusiasm for the T-shirts, Kristian Walsh interjects that the idea of the T-shirt wearing should have been taken out of the players' hands by the management of the club. Gareth Roberts also pans the wearing of the T-shirts and the statement from the club which defended the players for supporting their colleague.

John Gibbons brings the discussion back to Rob Gutmann's declaration of being on the wrong side of a noble cause. Alas, Gibbons is irritated by anti-racist groups. He claims:

"On the point that Rob said about the people going against us and how dangerous that is. Although I agree, I've been slightly annoyed by attitudes both in the press and anti-racism groups who have basically said 'well isn't it fantastic that someone is being done'. And you think 'well, no, not really' because well, it is if he's done it. But it seems to be it's great that he's been charged because 'we can show how strong we are against this subject', which is a problem. But since then a group's come out yesterday, a European anti-racism group in football, and said that 'they don't think that Liverpool should challenge it because it shows a bad example.'"

He persists with his opposition against groups who fight racism in Europe:

"I think if Liverpool football club think this is the wrong decision, then they've got a right to challenge it. Whether or not this is seen as an issue by some people who are doing good things."

Mike Girling returns to Gareth Roberts' point of LFC's legal team being under-prepared. He notes:

"What you have to remember in these incidents is it can be quite easy for the cards to be stacked against you, you know in terms of process, and you come out of it looking a c**t because maybe the other side have been better briefed than you have. And I think that's happened. I think Liverpool have got a decision to make here. Whether they go after the contents of the judgement or they go after the process, by which the judgement was made, has being inherently unfair."

He then moves onto the Kenneth Williams defence:

"There's a bigger picture which is basically saying the FA had it *in for us* from the start and therefore the process was [inaudible word] and made us look like c***s all the way through it."

Gareth Roberts brings a bit of sanity to proceedings by acknowledging that Suarez used a word he shouldn't have. Mike Girling isn't happy with Roberts' viewpoint and returns to the process, calling it:

"A f*****g farce."

Steve Graves, like Roberts, accepts-due to *probability*-why the FA could find Suarez guilty. Rob Gutmann is having none of it. He protests:

"I disagree 100% with that."

He goes on: "I think the probability issue is the one they've hung him on. Probability and credibility, they've hung him on probability. I think there are some clear facts. What is the likelihood of a man who's not angry because Suarez was not angry at that time? Evra was the one wound up about being kicked. In a crowded goalmouth..." [Gutmann is interrupted by Atkinson].

He chips in with:

"[...] Suarez was wound up with the coin toss."

Gutmann continues with his version of the truth:

"So, Suarez is calm and yet out of the blue, he's suddenly given a volley of five racist, not just used the word 'negro' in the testimony [...] they say he's basically used 'negro', as he's used n****r. 5 times he's used that unprovoked in a crowded goalmouth and no-one's heard it. What's the likelihood? And Evra has gone mental on the back of that. What is the probability of that being true?"

Jay McKenna has no sympathy for the victim. He contends:

"This is my issue with how Liverpool have handled the evidence. There's clear video footage that they've used to corroborate their augment. Liverpool could have easily used that to corroborate, to say, 'well okay, so if he's said n****r', at this point, as Patrice Evra believed he said at the time. Patrice Evra didn't think he said 'negro' or called him black. Patrice Evra felt that Luis Suarez had called him a 'n****r' and then he kept calling him it. So, look at his face as they used in one instant where he's pinched his skin or when he's firstly apparently said something to him or tapped him on the head."

He goes on:

"I watched him walk away from the referee, I watched in that goalmouth. He doesn't look like someone who's just called him a n****r and he wants to punch someone. He wanted to punch Suarez before that. So, if someone called him a 'n****r', why didn't he [head] butt him? Why hasn't he reacted angrily."

On this very point, Evra himself remarked:

"[...] Imagine if I punched him, in all the TV and all the kids would see me punching Luis Suarez, and I would have looked like the villain."[4]

Neil Atkinson backs up McKenna's account of the truth:

"And you've also got the footage where he's supposedly in shock, which is absolutely ridiculous. It verges on obscene."

Steve Martin comes back to his 'Sword of Damocles' T-shirt argument again:

"[...] Liverpool, I think did the right thing to come out with the T-shirts on and to put that statement out. Because I believe that their objective was to prove or to show that they don't believe Suarez is a racist. But I do think that Liverpool, from what I'm told, that Suarez has made a big mistake."

He then finds some sanity:

"Now, we are all saying that Evra was already wound up. If he is already wound up, use common sense, don't use a term that could wind him up even more. Suarez did and Suarez admitted that."

Gutmann can't have his man tainted.

"But did he use it innocently?"

Martin retorts with:

"No. No. If anyone believes that it was his intention to use that term innocently, then they are naïve."

Like Gutmann, Girling defends Suarez to the death:

"He's having a Spanish conversation."

Martin comes back with:

"The man was wound up, he made a reference to his skin colour. I don't believe, no matter if you're South American, North American, European or what, you don't do it. You know as soon as you signed a contract to play in this country, you don't do it. And for eleven of us white people to sit here and say, 'well what was Evra's interpretation of it'. I would love to say, 'What is a black person's interpretation of this and how would they have felt. And a black Liverpool fan.'"

The noise cranks up from the panellists because either they understand Martin is holding a mirror up to them, or because you simply cannot go against the club in any way, shape or form. Some of them are confused which is confirmed by Jay McKenna because he just puts words in a bingo machine and hopes it makes him sound like a decent human being:

"The point Steve's made is a good point [...] It's an offence. It's how you take it. I've looked at this from an amateur point of view. I've been a Trade Union representative representing someone before the idea of discrimination, harassment and bullying where if this was used in a workplace context in an office, it's how the offence was took. It doesn't also have to be the intended recipient. Patrice Evra could not have heard this supposedly, David de Gea who has seemingly heard nothing in a crowded goalmouth when you can hear everything from the Kop, has heard it. So, if he hears it and takes offence and believes that it's a racist slur he can go and make a subsequent complaint to [...]."[5]

AFTER A BRIEF DISCUSSION about the FA's possible intentions, Jay McKenna turns to the club's mistakes, he states:

"[...] This is where Liverpool should have been cleverer, [...] actually not even cleverer, Liverpool should have just said 'he's said this' and you know what in the cold light of day it looks terrible, but here's all are justification for it."[6]

Mike Girling is definitely confused by McKenna's use of "terrible". He also drops the Gregory Peck act:

"It doesn't look terrible [...] This is the worst possible f*****g case they could have taken for a racism charge for someone to get an 8-match ban because there's f**k all in it. Hardly anything, there's hardly any purgative words used and there's hardly anything that Suarez has said could be deemed has being really racially bad. And he's got an 8-match ban, 40,000 fine and career probably f*****g ruined in terms of sponsorship. He's got the whole of Europe calling him a racist."

Despite having purportedly read the report, Jay McKenna's back to his inventions by blaming the FA:

"They've looked at it and said you've made a reference to this fella's skin. Whereas, Liverpool could have come out and said all the stuff at the very beginning and Liverpool would have known the word he's used is 'negro', come out and put it out there. Whereas you've got the whole of Europe now calling him a racist, and he's got the media in this country believing the FA's spin on this because of all the PR that's gone on the other side of the argument."

This gives voice to Rob Gutmann, who insists:

"Jay, I think the problem is the word 'negro' has got 'ns' and 'gs' and a vowel in between them. So, in the west whatever we say rationally, we can't get past the fact that it sounds like the word 'n****r'. It's exactly like Steve said, 'come on at the end of the day, it is like the word 'n****r', so let's not kid ourselves and I understand that way of thinking."

In his own inimitable style, he moves back onto the finer points of language:

"Let's replace it with 'Jock or Ginge alright calm down,' you wouldn't go that was really ill-advised you can't do that, [...] where Suarez comes from in Uruguay, we're led to believe and I'm only going on what we're led to believe that that word in a huge percentage of cases is utterly benign."

Steve Martin replies to Gutmann with:

"Likewise, if there was a big Scottish man in front of me, who was really angry, I wouldn't say to him, 'What's the matter, Jock?'"

Normality finally hits Gutmann:

"Only because he'd hit you."

Martin tells Gutmann that's the whole point of the situation. Staying with the north of the border theme, Steve Graves states:

"On the point about Jock. If that charge had been brought before the FA, you would be guilty of a breach of that [...]."

Someone randomly says; "Strict liability basis." This sends Neil Atkinson off on one and the bingo machine is out again:

"On a strict liability basis what exactly do we actually, that's really interesting do we know of in criminal law which works on a strict liability basis there isn't many on the statute."

McKenna then puts himself in the place of Suarez by saying that when he was protesting against LFC's former American owners George Gillett and Tom Hicks, he described them as Yanks and basically Suarez did the same to Evra. Kristian Walsh then says the FA panel weren't qualified to make a decision because they, like the people in this podcast, are white. What he fails to have noticed, in spite of reading the report, is the FA panel took expert advice.

Gutmann's in like a flash:

"Exactly."

Walsh keeps up his argument:

"How did 3 dyed-in-the-wool Englishmen end up on the commission?"

Jay McKenna goes on a rant and finishes with:

"[...] I'll wait for the FA to send over a delegation to Uruguay and tell them they're a country full of racists for using 'negro' every now and again."[7]

He proceeds with his fume by claiming the FA are naïve. Atkinson then suggests the club should go down every possible route to correct the decision. McKenna backs up his colleague. Steve Graves insists Suarez should go down the defamation road. After more tirades, they then effortlessly move on to what Andy Carroll can bring to LFC as a centre-forward.

NINE

THERE'S MORE TO THE REPORT THAN MEETS THE EYE

Liverpool decided they would not appeal against Luis Suarez's ban, even though the striker again defended his actions and the club renewed their criticism of the English FA's disciplinary panel.[1] Liverpool's decision to accept the punishment meant the ban started with immediate effect, ruling the striker out of that evening's Premier League match at Manchester City and taking him out of action until February. Suarez said on his *Twitter* account:

"I will comply with the sanction, but with the acquiescence of someone who has not done anything and who feels extremely upset about what has transpired."[2]

The club itself stated:

"The (Football Association) panel has damaged the reputation of one the Premier League's best players, deciding he should be punished and banned for perhaps a quarter of a season."

Their denial of the situation went on: "Mr. Evra was deemed to be credible in spite of admitting that he himself used insulting and threatening words towards Luis and that his initial charge as to the word used was somehow a mistake [...]. The facts in this case were that an accusation was made, a rebuttal was given and there was video of the match. The remaining facts came from testimony of people who did not corroborate any accusation made by Mr. Evra."[3]

While insisting that Suarez did not "engage in a racist act," Liverpool said that they needed to move on from the episode. They claimed paradoxically:

"Continuing a fight for justice in this particular case beyond today would only obscure the fact that the club wholeheartedly supports the efforts... to put an end to any form of racism in English football."

Their statement continued in a contradictory manner: "It is time to put the Luis Suarez matter to rest and for all of us, going forward, to work together to stamp out racism in every form both inside and outside the sport."[4]

Liverpool also hinted that Manchester United launched the disciplinary action because they are a fierce rival of the Premier League champions. They proclaimed:

"This case has... provided a template in which a club's rival can bring about a significant ban for a top player without anything beyond an accusation."[5]

Without irony they went on to say they had "been a leader in taking a progressive stance on issues of race and inclusion" as part of an inclusive English game. Lacking in self-awareness they also stated:

"In far too many countries, the issues of racism and discrimination have been covered over or ignored."[6]

His teammates also released a statement defending their star striker. It read:

"Luis Suarez is our teammate and our friend and as a

group of players we are shocked and angered that he has been found guilty by the FA. We totally support Luis and we want the world to know that. We know he is not racist."

It proceeded with:

"We have lived, trained and played with Luis for almost 12 months and we don't recognise the way he has been portrayed. We will continue to support Luis through this difficult period, and as a popular and respected friend of all his teammates."

Cringingly, it finished with:

"[...] he will not walk alone."[7]

THE GAME against Manchester City gave the Reds their first opportunity to display their eagerness "to stamp out racism in every form, inside and outside the sport". It fell to Kenny Dalglish to deliver the message. In the after-match press conference, the Scot was asked:

"Kenny, the wider world is pretty shocked that, if a player can call someone 'negro' and the player who is the victim in this takes offence, that there is no apology or contrition offered from your club."[8]

Dalglish was in scornful mode again:

"I would have thought that, if you pronounced the word [negro] properly, you maybe understand it better. I think it was Spanish he was speaking, and I don't think you were speaking Spanish there."

The reporter obliged with a Spanish pronunciation: Dalglish said:

"Ask a linguistic expert, which certainly I am not. They will tell you that the part of the country in Uruguay where he comes from, it is perfectly acceptable. His wife calls him that and I don't think he is offended by her. We have made a statement and I think it is there for everybody to read. Luis has made a brilliant statement and we will stand by him."

The reporter came back with:

"But the FA verdict said it was 'simply incredible' to suggest it wasn't used in an offensive way when they were clearly arguing, and it wasn't friendly."

Dalglish retorted with a line of there's more to the report than meets the eye:

"There's a lot of things we'd like to say and a lot we could say but we would only get ourselves in trouble. We are not trying to be evasive [...] well, we are being evasive because we don't like getting ourselves in trouble. But we know what has gone on. We know what is not in the report and that's important for us. So, without me getting ourselves in trouble, I think that's it finished."

The press conference then moved onto the Wigan T-shirts. A journalist asked about any regrets the club may have. Dalglish carried on with his similar insinuations:

"You see, if one of you guys were in trouble, would you help him? Would you support him if you knew the truth and you knew it was right? Would you support him?"

The journalist responded with:

"But not with T-shirts when he has been found guilty [...]"

Dalglish came back with:

"Why not? If they want to show their support for their team-mate, what's wrong with that? It was a fabulous statement to make visually of their support for a guy who is endeared in the dressing room, one of their closest friends in the dressing room, and all of his friends in the dressing room can speak up adequately and perfectly well for him."

The Scot continued with his perceived ambiguities of the process:

"And I think it is very dangerous and unfortunate that you don't actually know the whole content of what went on at the hearing. I'm not prepared, and I can't say it, but I am just saying it is really unfortunate you never got to hear it. That's all I'm saying."

A reporter probed Dalglish:

"Kenny, given how the wider public are so opposed to your view, what do you have to lose by telling us and revealing what you're saying was not included in the FA statement?"

Dalglish was non-committal. He believed it was up to the club to decide what they want to do.

The reporter prodded more:

"But if you have something to say, surely say it – because the alternative is you are digging a bigger hole for yourself?"

Dalglish replied with:

"I don't think we are digging a bigger hole, but I just think it's unfortunate we can't be more forthcoming. That's the unfortunate thing."

A journalist then inquired:

"The hearing was to lay out all the evidence, 115 pages of evidence, and you have said they [the FA] have done it subjectively. So why do you think the FA are targeting Liverpool and Suarez?"

Dalglish responded with:

"Maybe wrong place, wrong time. It could have been anybody. I can't answer for the FA, you ask them."

Suarez's first game back was possibly and coincidently to be against Manchester United. A reporter asked:

"Are you concerned Suarez's first game back could be at Old Trafford?"

Dalglish had no such concerns:

"I'll just be delighted to get him back."[9]

For me, there is one main explanation why Kenny Dalglish was willing to come across as a defender of racism and unable to contemplate how much he was fanning the flames of racism. We will discuss this in *Chapters seventeen and eighteen*.

DALGLISH AND LFC'S attitude did not go down well with anti-racism campaigners. Lord Ouseley, who was head of the Commission for Racial Equality from 1993 to 2000, wrote:

"LFC need to take a hard look at themselves and how they have responded to the complaint and the investigations into the allegations of abuse in the Patrice Evra-Luis Suarez case. Throughout the entirety of the proceedings, over the past three months, all we have heard are denials and denigration of Evra. Since the publication of the 115-page report of the findings of the FA's independent commission, Liverpool's vitriol has increased. Suarez's attempt at a belated apology is nothing short of lamentable."[10]

He went on:

"I cannot believe that a club of Liverpool's stature, and with how it has previously led on matters of social injustice and inequality, can allow its integrity and credibility to be debased by such crass and ill-considered responses."

Lord Ouseley then moved on to what he saw as the club's duplicity:

"Liverpool have been particularly hypocritical. You

can't on the one hand wear a Kick It Out T-shirt in a week of campaigning against racism when this is also happening on the pitch: it's the height of hypocrisy. Liverpool players wore a T-shirt saying, 'We support Luis Suarez', seemingly whatever the outcome. This was a dreadful knee-jerk reaction because it stirs things up. And then, this was followed, after the verdict, with a kind of stance that says: 'Hey, we support anti-racism and Kick It Out. But we're not sorry. All we are really saying is that we blame someone else, not us.'"

Lord Ouseley then touched on the American owners, Fenway Sports Group:

"Surely the new owners, with their experiences of equality and inclusion in the US, can see how their brand is being devalued, and if they sanction this sort of lack of professionalism and moral leadership, we may as well pack up and go home and forget about anti-racism. The FA has shown that it has the bottle to back its Respect campaign by enforcing rules and regulations with regard to unacceptable behaviour and conduct. We have a duty and responsibility to demonstrate to the world how we deal with this issue. It's fine to criticise FIFA and UEFA but let's show we can take care of our own business. The future of football needs such strong and decisive leadership, especially for the next generation of young people who play the game across the country. Let's remove all racists and bigots from football."[11]

Despite the FA's findings, Rob Gutmann saw things differently to Ouseley. He put the blame on the victim. Gutmann, in a match report style, and with very little soul-searching, wrote:

"[...] Evra, who is wound up from the get-go about captaining his team in this key match, and who is extremely wary of a dangerous opponent in Luis Suarez. He will have known full well (before the outset) that the Uruguayan was the danger man that he and his fellow defenders had to stop. At all costs, it seems. The process starts in that moment just before the hour when he attempts to get Suarez disciplined by deceitful means (hugely exaggerating injury, as the video evidence clearly shows), and builds and builds from there."[12]

He went on:

"At the end of a difficult afternoon, Evra leaves the pitch a frustrated and angry player, aware that his team had finished a key game on the back foot, and that he as captain, had not acquitted himself with the dignity and composure required of his status. He knows that at some point Suarez used the word *'negro'* to him, and he cares little as to its intent or meaning but recognises enough *'n's'* and *'g's'* and vowels to lay an easy (faux) racism charge on Suarez. He suspects that he only needs a camera to have captured Suarez mouth *'negro'* and he's got the Liverpool forward bang to rights. If that happens, Evra is a clear victim, and quite possibly his yellow card would be rescinded as a consequence, and his petulant nervy performance put into a better light."

He finishes with:

"Evra then decamps from the fray on 90 minutes and within a short space of time has in frustration presented a picture of himself as the victim of abuse to colleagues and a French TV crew, rather than mentally disintegrating aggressor the match day cameras capture. Once he has set a pernicious train in motion there is little turning back for him or the unfortunate Suarez, who finds himself collateral damage in Evra's mind game."[13]

Over a decade later many people pointed out how racist some of Gutmann's thoughts came across in relation to Evra-Suarez. With this in mind, the *Anfield Wrap* deleted several of his articles, including this one. In the final part of the book, we are going to discuss in relative detail 3 theories why so many LFC fans would support a racist act. Additionally, we will very briefly mention a fourth concept in passing. For me, it is very straightforward to place most Reds into a particular theory, with Gutmann however, it's much trickier.

TEN

"PEOPLE MIGHT NOT REALISE THEY ARE RACIST."

On 6 January Liverpool defeated Oldham Athletic 5-1 in the third round of the FA Cup. Two days later Manchester United beat Manchester City 3-2 at the Etihad Stadium. No prizes for guessing who were drawn together in the fourth round.

After the Oldham match and LFC's decision not to appeal the ban the *Anfield Wrap* came out fighting. Hosting as usual is Neil Atkinson. The line-up had been tweaked a little, so the panel is made up of Jim Boardman, Peter Hooton, Kristian Walsh, Mike Girling, Rob Gutmann, and Paul Salt. Apart from the odd voice of sanity here and there, these men left their dignity on the steps of the studio.

Atkinson opens up by informing the audience that LFC had decided not to appeal the Suarez decision. Rob Gutmann begins the debate. He goes around the houses, but he seems happy that the club were still "defiant" in not appealing, but at the same time still defending their man. Atkinson introduces Peter Hooton to contribute by calling the situation a mess.

Hooton agrees. He underlines how significant it is that

you can't find one journalist, even Red supporting ones, who support the club's stance. He goes onto point out the LFC's legal representatives aren't "two-bit lawyers" as some people are trying to make out. He notes, however, that someone told him you wouldn't want them representing you in a court case when an accusation of racism was involved. Unsurprisingly, Mike Girling disagrees on the stance shout and backs the club to the hilt. He declares:

"[...] If you change that word 'stance' to 'approach', then I could agree with that. I think the club was in an invidious situation where they believe their man to be innocent, so their stance has got to be 'he's innocent first and foremost and we're going to fight that charge'".[1]

He proceeds by going after the victim:

"Now, the way they went about it you could argue has been at fault, but the actual stance I don't have a problem with. Maybe Liverpool were guilty of naivety because it became clear to most observers and Liverpool that this wasn't about Suarez v Evra, this was the FA v Suarez and Evra was the star witness."

Hooton disagrees with Girling in relation to who the fight is between. He perplexingly believes the fight is between Ferguson and Dalglish. He goes on to say that he's got no problems with Dalglish supporting his player, but he does criticise the confrontational approach. Next, like Girling, Rob Gutmann, attacks the injured party. He contends:

"Evra raised the bar with his 10 times claim on day one."

Atkinson notes that Evra has not been held to the same level of criticism or scrutiny as Suarez. Paul Salt concurs with Atkinson, he suggests:

"That's a really good point because if you read all the

media coverage [...] it has been very one-sided. And there hasn't been much reporting about Liverpool's problem with the case and why Liverpool are so upset about it. Kenny even said last week 'I would like to tell you, but I can't because I don't want to go before the FA again' [...]."

Salt goes on:

"And I think I've probably only read one article about why Liverpool are so upset and that is because that is if you read the article, it's the fact that Evra could rely on video evidence when Suarez couldn't and things like that, but a lot of people don't know that."

Next to comment is Girling. He just puts chunks of language together which make little or no sense, he says of journalists; "[...] they don't want to look under the covers because they mightn't like what they find."[2] The paranoia and irrationality continue as they throw the usual subjects into the mix, such as; the FA, the FA panel, LFC's legal representation, LFC not getting a fair hearing, LFC's PR department, internal civil war within LFC, Manchester United's influence, and other clubs, for example, Chelsea, manipulating the media. One of them even claims absurdly that they went into "a sword fight with a baguette." Gutmann believes "[...] we are guilty of a lack of guile."

THEY THEN MOVE on to a racist incident which took place at Anfield at the Oldham FA cup game. Hooton mentioned that T-shirts were on sale outside the ground in defence of the Uruguayan. He then claims that he sympathises with Liverpool fans who have supported Suarez because "[...]. He probably hasn't done much wrong. He's been a victim of circumstances and a victim of legislation and the rules of the FA."

Hooton's clarity of mind resurfaces because he continues with:

"But when you get the club who look like they are prevaricating on condemning racism, you get an atmosphere where it was inventible to me that Friday was going to happen."

Atkinson isn't happy with Hooton's lucidity. He tells him:

"I'm going to push on this."

He goes onto claim, despite himself stoking the fire for months, that "inevitable" is a really strong word and that the atmosphere in the stadium was a bit of a "wool" mood. Gutmann then blames the press for young LFC fans behaving abhorrently and then (if we aren't already), we are into the land of utter gobbledegook. He comes out with these sentences:

"You can't have this McCarthyism approach [...]." And: "It's the press making this into the latest X-Factor [...]."

Jim Boardman then asserts that some people might not realise they are racist. I agree with him. After this, the conversation becomes so muddled with Atkinson and Hooton quarrelling with one another. Hooton goes on to claim the club has been exposed, not because of what Suarez said but because of their lack of media savvy. Gutmann returns to his expertise of South American linguistics, alleging that Suarez's vocabulary was equal to "Bro."

Hooton brings some reasoning to proceedings by pointing out that Suarez's language was used during a heated argument which he could physically see himself from the Kop. Gutmann interrupts to maintain Suarez may be saying:

"Calm down pal," or "Aright mate, watch yourself!"

Girling then alleges that Manchester United were being pernicious after the game by going after Suarez. Hooton agrees with Girling. Hooton suggests that Liverpool have fallen into the trap and that it's like lemmings going over the cliff. Atkinson then brings up the possibility of "Peace Talks" before the cup tie between the two giants.

As you can image the conversation descended further into farce. A few 'highlights' are Mike Girling contending that "The ones who are a little bit racist, are going to be a little bit racist".[3] Like with Boardman, he's not wrong.

Next, some panellists get their defence in first by stating that if Evra's booed in the forthcoming FA cup game against Manchester United at Anfield, it's not to do with racism, therefore nobody could criticise LFC fans for being racist. They start blaming the FA for the damage that could be done to anti-racism campaigns if LFC fans boo Evra. So, let me try to comprehend this. They are saying LFC fans booing Evra is okay and it's the FA who are forcing them to do it? I think that's right, but these podcasts are really hard to fathom.

Next was this defence which I'm surprised took so long to appear. It came from Kristian Walsh:

"Liverpool's a multicultural city. It welcomes anyone as long as you don't wear a jester hat. Seriously, it's a wonderful city in my opinion. It's a very multicultural cosmopolitan city and the idea from the media that we're this archaic, you know snarling..." [his voice fades].

Neil Atkinson weighs in with:

"It's a South-East fiction [...] whilst ignoring John Terry [...]."

Just staying with Kristian Walsh's point for a moment. He clearly cannot see the irony of how parochial he and his fellow panellists are. Norwich City fan, Janice Allen-Brade, would definitely have disagreed with Walsh. She said:

"I am a football fan; I have lived in Liverpool for 14 years and I am black. The controversy over the racist abuse case between Luis Suarez and Patrice Evra has made me rethink my feelings towards the city and Liverpool supporters."

She also underscored something Walsh and his colleagues were blinded to (Steve Martin excluded):

"But that is nothing compared to the dilemmas faced by Liverpool's black fans. In all the debate about this issue their perspective has been overlooked."

Unlike the *Anfield Wrap* Allen-Brade noted:

"Personally, I have taken to avoiding conversations on the issue because I find the lengths people will go to rationalise Suarez's behaviour depressing. It is far more upsetting than the initial offence."[4]

Returning to the show, after twenty-five minutes of the group psychosis, the conversation, without breaking sweat moves onto midfielder Jonjo Shelvey.

SEVERAL YEARS later Neil Atkinson appeared on a different podcast. When confronted about his support for Suarez, he responded with:

"Yes, not overtly, not crazily."[5]

When I listened to this my first thought was:

"Thank God he and his colleagues didn't support Suarez 'overtly and crazily'. God only knows what they would have come out with if they had".

Just to summarise their podcasts. They reminded me of Boris Johnson's cabinet, when for a few years during scandal after scandal, they appeared on Breakfast TV. They came out with some of the most absurd excuses imaginable to defend their leader. In the end, history has shown it all became too humiliating and Johnson was eventually forced out of office.

At the end of the day, you cannot defend the indefensible with rational debate. Neil Atkinson, Jim Boardman, Giulio Canetti, John Gibbons, Mike Girling, Steve Graves, Rob Gutmann, Andy Heaton, Peter Hooton, Jay McKenna, Steve Martin and Kristian Walsh have all proved that.

ON 28 JANUARY Liverpool won the fourth-round tie 2-1. The game seemed destined for a reply when Ji-Sung Park's powerful shot brought United level after Daniel Agger had put Liverpool into the lead-but Dirk Kurt had other ideas and his late goal sent the Kop into raptures. The background to the game was, of course, October's incident. The calls for calm from both camps fell on death ears in thousands of cases as Evra was subjected to constant jeering and taunts throughout - along with vociferous claims from Liverpool fans that, to phrase this politely, his evidence in the case was less than reliable.[6]

Sympathy was certainly in short supply for Evra and his quest for justice. The next day, Gareth Roberts played down the abuse Evra had to withstand. He penned an article entitled "Who's arsed?", clearly Roberts wasn't. His piece contended:

"Booing Evra is racist? Ok, if you say so. Who's arsed what you've got to say?"[7]

As cold and as entrenched as Roberts' commentary appears, another Red went much further. The Red was arrested after television viewers spotted him making a monkey gesture in the stands during the match. The fan denied two counts of using abusive or insulting words within the hearing or sight of a person likely to be caused alarm or distress.

During the trial, the court was shown footage of the incident and also heard evidence from fellow Liverpool fans who sat near him in the lower Centenary Stand and heard him direct racist slurs at Evra and Manchester United supporters. The Red tried to explain away the gesture as a reference to 'cavemen' and also claimed he was unaware of the connotations of an expression he had used. He was found guilty of the two charges. The chair of the bench, Ray Moore, said both the gesture and comment were 'clearly racist'. The supporter was fined £180 and handed a four-year banning order that prevented him from attending Liverpool and England matches or entering Liverpool city centre for four hours before kick-off and after the final whistle.[8]

PART FOUR
HANDSHAKE

ELEVEN
"BANG OUT OF ORDER."

After serving his 8-match ban, Suarez returned for Liverpool in a 0-0 draw against Tottenham on 6 February. On 11 February Liverpool played Manchester United at Old Trafford. The hope was everything would be about the football. Patrice Evra certainly wanted it to be about the football. He commented:

"It was unbelievable all week. [...] It was like the handshake was more important than Manchester United versus Liverpool, a massive game. So that's why I was frustrated because I wanted people to focus on the game."

On a more personal level, he noted: "My mum asked me what I was going to do. I told her that I am the sort of person who would forgive. So I would shake his hand no matter what. He made a mistake. I won't go on holiday with him, but I will shake his hand."[1]

At the press conferences for the game, Alex Ferguson drew a contrast between the response of the two clubs to the episode, however, and queried Liverpool's reluctance to launch an appeal over the punishment given Dalglish's firm belief that Suarez should not have been banned[2]. Dalglish remarked:

"It is fantastic to have him [Suarez] back. He should never have been out in the first place."[3]

Ferguson responded:

"Well, why didn't they appeal? I think we would be better putting that to bed. We have plenty of other important issues to be concentrating on, like chasing City in the league and preparing for the Europa League games."

He also observed: "We'll just get on with the job and concentrate on the game. They [Liverpool] have said plenty, haven't they? But we've kept our own counsel, because we thought that was the right thing to do in these situations."[4]

Ferguson had written in his programme notes that his "biggest regret is the way Patrice has been castigated in some quarters for standing up to racism".[5] On the day of the match during the pre-game interviews, the Scot stressed:

"If you get a good game, it transcends everything. I think we want to see good football. Both clubs have great histories, and a good game would do [everyone] the world of good."[6]

Unfortunately, Ferguson and football didn't get their wish.

During the traditional pre-match handshake, the Uruguayan forward refused to greet Evra by pulling his hand away from the Frenchman. Referee, Phil Dowd, had to intervene. After Suarez ignored his teammate, Manchester United's Rio Ferdinand refused to shake Suarez's. Evra declared:

"When I went to shake his hand and I saw he didn't, I was like, 'what's wrong with that guy?' He made himself worse. He made himself worse. And I am feeling sad for him."[7]

The Manchester United player's sadness turned to anger. He thought Suarez's attitude was a disgrace and he wanted to 'kill' the Uruguayan. During the match he even tackled Rio Ferdinand by mistake trying to get to the Liverpool forward. He said:

"I didn't want to play the game. I wanted to kill him."[8]

UNFORTUNATELY, the non-handshake led to an undercurrent throughout a match which was won by two goals from Wayne Rooney inside the first four minutes of the second half. Suarez pulled a goal back late on, but it was too little too late. The goals and the result were secondary. Just before half-time Suarez became involved in another flashpoint. He was left irate after he deemed, he had been fouled by Ferdinand. The Uruguayan castigated the officials before kicking the ball towards the crowd as the half-time whistle sounded.

As the players left the field for half-time Suarez was roundly booed by the home fans. There was also an air of ill-feeling between the players which spilled over into the tunnel. It was reported that Evra was trying to confront Suarez. As the players got to the entrance of the dressing rooms, Liverpool's Slovakian defender, Martin Skrtel, blocked Evra's path and that was the cue for players from both sides to get involved. There was a lot of pushing and shoving with police and stewards involved. It took around 5 minutes for players to eventually reach their dressing rooms.

Like we said before, the game finished 2-1 to the home side, but there was plenty of drama to come. Phil Dowd had to intervene at the Stretford End as Patrice Evra milked the celebrations directly in front of Suarez. With tempers fraying, players from both sides became involved in pushing and shoving. The Frenchman was kept on the pitch whilst the other players headed down the tunnel. The home side put the blame squarely on the Uruguayan. Alex Ferguson didn't hold back:

"He's a disgrace to Liverpool Football Club. The player should not be allowed to play for Liverpool again. The history that club's got and he does that. In a situation like today, he could have caused a riot. I was really disappointed in that guy. That was terrible what he did."[9]

The Liverpool boss held a different view to his Scottish counterpart. Dalglish became embroiled in an undignified interview with Sky Sports reporter Geoff Shreeves. Shreeves first asks:

"What's your reaction to Luis Suarez refusing to shake Patrice Evra's hand? And did you have an inkling that he was going to do that?"[10]

The Liverpool boss replied that he didn't know about the refusal to shake hands because he wasn't there and that it was contrary to what he'd been told. Shreeves persists with:

"Now that I have told you Kenny, what's your reaction to that?"

The Reds boss says:

"We'll ask him and take it from there."

Shreeves then enquires:

"Do you think you have to take a serious look at his refusal to shake his hand and the way it subsequently set the tone for elements of what happened here today?"

An incensed Dalglish replies with:

"I think you're very severe. Bang out of order to blame Luis Suarez for anything that happened here today. Right, I think today predominately both sets of fans behaved really well. They had a little banter with each other, no problem."

Dalglish then asks Shreeves how many bookings there were in the game. Shreeves tells Dalglish that he's not talking about the fans. Gesturing with his arm, Dalglish informs him he can leave the interview at any time he wants. Shreeves tells Dalglish that there was controversy in the tunnel; that police and stewards were called before and after the game because of the tension and the "no handshake" incident.

Dalglish then insinuates that the controversy might have been stoked by Sky's 24-hour rolling TV build up to the match. He points out that their the FA Cup tie from January did not have problems because it was screened by a different station. The interview finishes with Dalglish again saying he had witnessed nothing personally.[11]

RIO FERDINAND, who snubbed Suarez's handshake after the Liverpool player had rejected Evra's, told MUTV:

"After seeing what happened, I decided not to shake his hand. I lost all respect for the guy. He has not got the respect that he needs to acknowledge he's made a mistake and say sorry and move on from that. It could have been resolved between the two players today. After this, it's not great."[12]

Alan Hansen, the former Liverpool captain, said on the BBC's *Match of the Day*:

"The rhetoric from both clubs before the game was restraint. Liverpool said there would be a handshake, so for Suarez to snub Evra is totally unacceptable. Liverpool have given Suarez total support through thick and thin and I think he's let Kenny down, he's let the club down and he's let himself down."[13]

The *Guardian's* Daniel Taylor picked-up on Dalglish's conduct:

"In the end, it was difficult to know what was the more depressing and shocking: that moment when Luis Suarez walked past Patrice Evra, refused to shake his hand and reminded us this is a man whose brains are all in his feet, or afterwards when Kenny Dalglish tried to stare down the questions before coming up with a response that was so outlandishly flawed it made you wonder where he was storing all the qualities which we once associated with him?[14]

TWELVE
"APOLOGIES WERE NECESSARY."

After months of disobedience, the non-handshake was the straw that broke the camel's back. Both Suarez and Dalglish's behaviour was eventually taken to task by embarrassed owners and sponsors. Both men were forced to make formal apologies for the conduct during the match against Manchester United. As the BBC reported, they [the BBC] subsequently learnt that the apologies "contained the input" of the club's American owners, Fenway Sports Group. "No one is more important than the club. Apologies were necessary," said a senior source at Fenway. The owners also believed Suarez could salvage his Liverpool career by demonstrating "better judgement"[1] in future.

As well as the owners, Standard Chartered, Liverpool's shirt sponsor, went public with its criticism. A brief statement read:

"We were very disappointed by Saturday's incident and have discussed our concerns with the club."

A person familiar with the matter said:

"It was a very robust conversation."[2]

With their careers now in jeopardy, both Suarez and Daglish 'miraculously' changed tack. Suarez stated:

"I have spoken with the manager since the game at Old Trafford and I realise I got things wrong. I have not only let [Dalglish] down but also the club and what it stands for and I'm sorry. I made a mistake and I regret what happened. I should have shaken Patrice Evra's hand before the game and I want to apologise for my actions. I would like to put this whole issue behind me and concentrate on playing football."[3]

Dalglish said:

"All of us have a responsibility to represent this club in a fit and proper manner. That applies equally to me as Liverpool manager. When I went on TV after yesterday's game, I hadn't seen what had happened, but I did not conduct myself in a way befitting of a Liverpool manager during that interview, and I'd like to apologise for that."

Manchester United announced:

"Manchester United thanks Liverpool for the apologies issued following Saturday's game. Everyone at Old Trafford wants to move on from this. The history of our two great clubs is one of success and rivalry unparalleled in British football. That should be the focus in the future of all those who love the clubs."

Liverpool managing director Ian Ayre also released a statement, which read:

"We are extremely disappointed Luis Suarez did not shake hands with Patrice Evra before yesterday's game. The player had told us beforehand that he would, but then chose not to do so. He was wrong to mislead us and wrong not to offer his hand to Patrice Evra. He has not only let himself down but also Kenny Dalglish, his teammates and the club."

He continued:

"It has been made absolutely clear to Luis Suarez that his behaviour was not acceptable. Luis Suarez has now apologised for his actions, which was the right thing to do. However, all of us have a duty to behave in a responsible manner and we hope he now understands what is expected of anyone representing Liverpool Football Club."

Dalglish added:

"Ian Ayre has made the club's position absolutely clear and it is right that Luis Suarez has now apologised for what happened at Old Trafford. To be honest, I was shocked to hear that the player had not shaken hands having been told earlier in the week that he would do."[4]

PFA chief executive Gordon Taylor described Suarez's conduct as "disrespectful, inappropriate and embarrassing".[5] Lord Ouseley said Dalglish's behaviour had "damaged" the club's reputation. He told *BBC Radio 5*:

"I'm delighted it's [the apology] happened, it's long overdue. The brand of Liverpool is built on success and dignity but it has been damaged, particularly by Kenny Dalglish's behaviour during the past few months."[6]

Then Sports Minister, Hugh Robertson, told *Sky Sports News*:

"There is an issue that still needs to be tackled. It goes beyond racism – you hear vile chanting about managers and opposition players. I don't think that really has any place in modern society. If we don't accept it on the high street, I see no reason why we should accept it in a football crowd."[7]

THIRTEEN
"THE BARBARIANS ARE AT OUR GATES."

In relation to the handshake and running contrary to people who were supporting the anti-racism line, Andy Heaton wrote the following:

"Man found guilty of a charge he feels he is innocent of by an organisation with a 99.5% conviction rate. Man is aggrieved at being found guilty and the subsequent ban imposed. Man not too keen on shaking hands with his accuser who he feels is responsible for his eight-game ban. Och, the mock indignation, the faux outrage, burn him, burn him as a witch."

Heaton also turned his displeasure towards Alex Ferguson. He commented:

"Then you have the biggest hypocrite of them all, Mr Ferguson, whose anger on the subject turned his nose a purpler shade of puce as he raged."[1]

Next, Heaton aimed his disapproval at *Guardian* journalist Daniel Taylor. He took offence because Taylor had tweeted:

"Always supported fanzine network – still miss picking

up my Brian from Selectadisc – police over-reaction re Red Issue spoof today."[2]

The tweet included the front page of a Manchester United fanzine that had a picture of a KKK hood and the words: "LFC Suarez is innocent".

The over-reaction Taylor referred to was that Greater Manchester Police asked the fanzine people to stop selling copies. Heaton saw his opportunity to deflect. He wrote:

"Of course, it's all a big joke, the Ku-Klux Klan and the brutal murder of black teens, church bombings and campaign of organised lynchings is something to be made fun of – 'Klanfield' t-shirts, ho-ho, how funny, how clever."

I think it is fair comment to say that any rational British person would understand that the guys at the fanzine were not making jokes about the suffering of black people at the hands of the KKK. They were joking about people such as Heaton. And I would add, he knows it.

In addition, Heaton declared:

"Greater Manchester Police, fortunately, took a more dim view and confiscated every copy of the magazine on the grounds of 'Inciting Racial Hatred'."[3]

Given his missives and the language he came out with, Heaton's accusation of others "Inciting Racial Hatred" is preposterous. It was undoubtedly a case of pot and kettle. Soon, we will see the consequences of "Inciting Racial Hatred" can have on people's lives.

BY 14 FEBRUARY, it had been two months since Rob Gutmann had participated in the initial *Anfield Wrap* broadcast. At this stage, Dalglish and Suarez had both apologised, although it would seem not to Evra. So, was Gutmann ready to do the same? The simple answer is "no". In fact, his views went the other way and they heightened. He wrote a piece that has since been removed. His opening gambit was:

"The last time I felt anything remotely like this as a Liverpool supporter was 27 years ago. 39 people had died at the 1985 European Cup final in Brussels, and Liverpool fans were blamed for their deaths. To this day I am none the wiser as to where precisely the true weight of culpability lay for the Heysel disaster, but I know that my club ultimately took responsibility for it, and that we as supporters remain haunted by the spectre of those events to this day."

He proceeded with the following:

"Heysel was about life and death. It was more important than an argument between two millionaire athletes, and the loyalties of two warring tribes. The Suarez and Evra mess, though, has come to echo 1985, for me at least, because there are parallels in terms of the sheer momentum of shame being foisted upon what felt then, and still feels now, like our family."

He went on to note: "The time for magnanimity in this affair is over. The barbarians are at our gates and the bridge has to come up. If no one likes us, then how can we care?"[4]

Who are the barbarians Gutmann is speaking of? Are they fellow LFC fans who were embarrassed by the club's behaviour? Or in particular black LFC fans?

One black LFC fan, Jeff Wiltshire, felt so strongly about the issue he stopped supporting Liverpool altogether. Wiltshire stated:

"When I saw Evra's reaction, I knew something serious had happened – as only a black person would. I could accept Liverpool's initial response. I think most employees would want the same reaction from their employer. But as it became more and more clear the allegations against Suarez had foundation, I became increasingly disgusted by the club's reaction. I haven't been able to watch them since. Kenny Dalglish, once my idol, has let me down."[5]

Ronnie Doforo, who we mentioned in the *Introduction*, remarked:

"[...] I feel more let down by the club than by what Suarez said. Though I remain a loyal supporter, as a black fan, I now see the club in a different light."[6]

As we will see in the next chapter, the 'barbarians' Gutmann and the *Anfield Wrap* were willing to go to the mattresses against, were; International, National and Local Black Organisations, Merseyside TUC, North-West Unite Against Fascism, the Society of Black Lawyers and the National Black Police Association.

FOURTEEN
UNITED AGAINST FASCISM

On 20 February Black community groups from Merseyside accused LFC of inciting racism through the handling of the affair.[1] The club were the subject of an open letter signed by members of the Liverpool Black Leadership Forum. The forum included consultant Gloria Hyatt, Eric Lynch from Slavery History Tours, and Femi Sowande from Merseyside Black History Month Group. Also involved were Paul Jenkins from North West Unite Against Fascism, Peter Herbert from the Society of Black Lawyers, the National Black Police Association and Merseyside TUC.

They highlighted that LFC actions, in vehemently rejecting the findings of the FA inquiry, the club's public displays of support for a player found guilty of racist abuse and his subsequent refusal to shake the hand of Evra at Old Trafford were completely unacceptable. The group considered therefore that these actions could be considered as inciting racial intolerance.

Whilst the subsequent apologies for the failure to engage with the traditions of a pre-game 'handshake' were welcomed by the group, they judged that there remained deep concern about LFC's absolute refusal to accept the findings of the FA's investigation. With this in mind, they deemed that such apologies failed to meet the test of genuine remorse and understanding. This was further negated by LFC's failure to apologise for racism either through the club or Suarez. They emphasised that neither had LFC recognised or acknowledged the consequent damage to race relations resulting from their actions and recognised by many people of all races across the country. And, as a result, efforts to combat racism in football and the wider society had been critically undermined.

Lastly, there was criticism of civic leaders in the city. It was noted that many civic leaders had remained silent on these critical issues and had failed to publicly condemn LFC's decision not to robustly and effectively challenge racism.[2]

Further to the letter, Gloria Hyatt, MBE, of the Liverpool Black Leadership Forum, observed:

"Liverpool Football Club has presided over the worst incident of racism in football seen in recent years. Their misguided handling of Suarez-Evra has let down all of those in the city who worked hard to challenge racism and make Liverpool a better place to live for everyone."[3]

Lee Jasper, a human rights and race equality campaigner, added:

"The club, including the owners, the players and the manager, need to realise the enormous damage caused by their reluctance and obdurate behaviour. Kenny Dalglish used to manage Celtic; he ought to know the importance of stamping out bigotry. The club failed the city, the nation as a whole and in particular Britain's black communities. Their abysmal lack of leadership on this issue has given a green light to racism. They must make urgent repetitions and make a clear and unequivocal apology."[4]

ON 24 FEBRUARY Gloria Hyatt wrote an essay in a national newspaper. She stressed Liverpool has the oldest black community in Europe, dating back more than two and a half centuries with many present before the city's trading of slaves. She noted that race-relations had historically been fraught, marked by significant events such as the 1919 riots, racial murders, and the 1981 uprisings of black and white communities over police harassment. Thankfully, she underlined things had been improving recently. However, there was a *but* in what she said next.

She remarked that LFC's handling of the Suarez-Evra affair was a defining moment in the city's history. She observed that there was deep unease about how the club had handled the original incident and its aftermath, and many residents were concerned that the club's actions may encourage racism. Heartbreakingly, she pointed out that local black people had endured vile and offensive racial abuse by Liverpool fans; this included the name Suarez being used to taunt people with black or brown skin. One local woman, Jane, reported that an acquaintance started a tirade of racial slurs against Evra, not realising she was a black woman due to her fair complexion. Another man told Hyatt that bananas were repeatedly thrown into his garden and that local youths were walking around his neighbourhood with Suarez masks on.[5]

With this happening, Hyatt wrote to Dalglish to raise these concerns, giving pointers on how to resolve this situation. But her letter was ignored.[6] This led to her participating in the group letter we mentioned previously. This time the club did write back.

But as Hyatt noted its response merely established the fact that they had learned little since the FA found Suarez had racially abused Evra. The club pointed out that Suarez had apologised to anyone he offended, but it ignored the fact he had not at that point apologised directly to Evra, nor had he yet done so for the racial abuse. As Hyatt went onto point out the club also failed to acknowledge that even Dalglish's apology appeared to be purely for the handshake incident.

Hyatt then highlighted that by failing to provide robust anti-racist leadership, the club had let down many of its fans, both black and white. In a city that is home to a rich cultural mix of indigenous and migrant communities from a wide variety of backgrounds, she believed clear leadership on this issue was critical.[7]

Unfortunately for Hyatt, in taking up the issue she felt a backlash, mainly through abusive phone calls and emails, and accusations that her consortium's intervention had made things worse. Of her tormentors she said:

"Let sleeping dogs lie, they say. The problem with that is the dogs of racism never sleep."[8]

Patrice Evra was also on the sharp end of racist torment. The day after the initial incident in October 2011, Evra didn't expect what was about to be unleashed. People were claiming he was a liar, and prisoners in Liverpool jails began sending him threatening letters saying they were going to kill him when they came out of prison. People on the outside of prison started following his car, so it became necessary for him to have 24-hour security for 3 months. His family were scared, Evra himself was less concerned, his outlook was:

"Guys, we don't need that because we're from the streets. So come on, we don't need protection."

But as he explained, the threats were real so that's why Manchester United said: "Patrice, if you don't need it, we need it. So, for 3 months [it was] unbelievable.[9]

PART FIVE
THE REASONS WHY

FIFTEEN

FOOD FIGHTS

Over the next few chapters, we will discuss why any LFC fan who was raised in the UK would have backed Suarez. For me there are three main reasons for this, additionally there is the fourth one that Gloria Hyatt spoke of, i.e., out-and-out racism. There is no question your genuine racist took advantage of the situation. A few blatant examples were the fan who was arrested at Anfield and the people who threw bananas into someone's garden. On top of this, there are supporters who could camouflage their racism by writing articles, appearing in podcasts, booing Evra in the stadium, and by chanting:

"Oh, Oh, Oh, Luis Suarez. His first name is Patrice, is Patrice, is Patrice, his second name is Evra, is Evra, is Evra and he's a f*****g liar, a liar, a liar and that's why we hate him, we hate him, we hate him. Oh, Oh, Oh, Luis Suarez [...]."

However, I believe the vast majority of Reds who backed Suarez fall into 3 other categories. The first group is Intergroup Behaviour (tribalism). The second is "modern racism" as opposed to the unconcealed one Hyatt speaks of.

And the final one is connected to the roots of LFC, and those origins mean the club itself and large portions of the fan base on occasions cannot see the woods for the trees.

Let's begin with the first. We can understand intergroup behaviour as the idea that:

"Whenever individuals belonging to one group interact, collectively or individually, with another group or its members in terms of their group identification, we have an instance of intergroup behaviour."[1]

Therefore, struggles between nations, political groups or football fans are all illustrations of intergroup behaviour. In terms of football rivalries there aren't too many bigger ones than Liverpool vs Manchester United. One of the classic concepts of intergroup behaviour is that of "ethnocentrism". In 1906, William Sumner was the first to use the term, together with those of "ingroup" and "outgroup".[2] For Sumner, ethnocentrism was a "syndrome" in the sense that it encompassed "a number of (mutually related) attributes of social life"; it played a function in group formation and intergroup competition, and it was universal. Sumner described ethnocentrism like this:

"A view of things in which one's own group is the centre of everything, and all others are scaled and rated with reference to it. Each group nourishes its own pride and vanity, boasts itself superior, exalts its own divinities, and looks with contempt on outsiders. Each group thinks its own folkways the only right one. Ethnocentrism leads a people to exaggerate and intensify everything in their own folkways which is peculiar and which differentiates them from others."[3]

One of the first landmark studies of intergroup behaviour was carried out by Muzafer Sherif. During his youth in what is now Turkey, Sherif witnessed interethnic violence between Turks, Greeks and Armenians that claimed tens of thousands of lives, and these experiences inspired him to seek answers to prevent further atrocities occurring in the future.[4] He conducted three famous field experiments in 1949, 1953 and 1954 at summer camps for young boys in the United States.[5]

When the boys arrived at camp, they were divided into two groups. The groups were separated from one another and then later brought together to participate in sporting and other activities. This produced passionate competition and intergroup antagonism and aggression, while at the same time manufacturing camaraderie within the groups themselves. During Sherif's trials, basically all intergroup activities deteriorated into intergroup conflicts. For example, when the groups dined together, the meals turned into an opportunity for the groups to fling food at each other. Intergroup rivalry became so vicious that a lot of the experiments were cancelled.

THE RESEARCH we are now going to turn to shows conflict is not even necessary to stir up intergroup behaviour, which makes the attitude of many Reds towards Evra even easier to understand.

In 1971, Henri Tajfel and his colleagues (Billig, Bundy and Flament) devised a novel way to demonstrate what has become known as minimal group paradigm. The aim of the study was to assess the effects of social categorisation on intergroup behaviour when, in the intergroup situation, neither calculations of individual interest nor previously existing attitudes of hostility could have been said to have determined discriminative behaviour against an outgroup.[6] In short, Tajfel et al. were attempting to show that you do not need prior hostility between groups for prejudice and conflict to occur. Therefore, it was a move away from earlier conflict theories such as Sherif's.

Tajfel's et al.'s research used Bristol schoolboys who believed they were taking part in a study on decision making. They carried out a pilot study and two subsequent studies. During their second experiment, the criterion for intergroup categorisation was adopted by using the paintings of artists Paul Klee and Wassily Kandinsky. Twelve coloured slides were chosen, six being reproductions of paintings by Klee and six by Kandinsky, all of which were fairly abstract. The participants were informed that they would be asked to express their preference between paintings of "two foreign modern painters, Klee and Kandinsky".

The slides were shown one at a time, in 12 successive pairs and in various combinations, without the participants being informed which of them were reproductions of Klee and which of Kandinsky. After each pair, the participants were requested to tick their preference on prepared answer sheets and were then placed into groups based on their preferences.

When you think about it, what is significant is that Klee and Kandinsky were modern artists, so it is not pushing the boundaries of the imagination to say the boys were more interested in the Gas and the Robins than painters from Switzerland and Russia, and so, therefore, the groups they joined were meaningless in their importance.

During the experiment, the boys only knew which group they belonged to and so had no idea as to the identity of outgroup and fellow ingroup members, who were masked by the use of code numbers. The boys went into private booths where they were presented with a matrix where they had to assign monetary value to either an ingroup or an outgroup member. They did not assign this monetary value to themselves; therefore, their own greed did not come into play. The most powerful force found in the study was ingroup favouritism, i.e., participants wanted to make sure that their group got more than the other group. In fact, the most chosen monetary value was the maximum difference between the ingroup and the outgroup.

There was also a tendency to choose fairness, but there wasn't a propensity to distribute money and give it to the outgroup. As Tajfel et al. note themselves, the main finding confirmed in all three experiments is clear: in a situation devoid of the usual trappings of ingroup membership and of all the vagaries of interacting with an outgroup, the participants still act in terms of their ingroup membership and of intergroup categorisation. Their actions unambiguously favour the members of their ingroup against the members of the outgroup. This happens despite the fact that an alternative strategy—acting in terms of the greatest common good—is clearly open to them at a relatively small cost of advantages that would accrue to members of the ingroup.

Two further aspects of the findings are even more important. First, the participants act in this way in a situation in which their own individual benefit is not affected one way or another. And second, as was shown in the second experiment and in the pilot experiment, when the participants have a choice between acting in terms of maximum utilitarian advantage to all (Maximum Joint Profit) combined with maximum utilitarian advantage to members of their own group (Maximum Ingroup Profit) as against having their group win on points at the sacrifice of both these advantages, it is the winning that seems more important to them.

Tajfel et al. conclude that the crucial results of the study can be simply restated as follows:

"[...] in a situation in which the participants' own interests were not involved in their decisions, in which alternative strategies were available that would maximise the total benefits to a group of boys who knew each other well, they acted in a way determined by an *ad hoc* intergroup categorisation."[7]

According to Tajfel, the finding that intergroup discrimination can be caused by a "minimal" social categorisation retains a considerable robustness. A count made for his review resulted in a conservative estimate of at least 30 studies which used minimal or near-minimal categorisations with diverse populations of participants, independent variables and dependent measures, and which all show ingroup-favouring bias.[8] Likewise, Hogg and Vaughan suggest the robust findings from hundreds of minimal group experiments conducted with a wide range of participants are that the mere fact of being categorised as a group member seems sufficient to produce ethnocentrism and competitive intergroup behaviour.[9]

SIXTEEN

MODERN RACISM

As we mentioned in a previous chapter, the Red who was arrested at Anfield and possibly the person at the *Anfield Wrap* who wrote, *"Suarez Reaction: The lads discuss the absolute f*****g abomination of a case against Luis Suarez and the witch-hunt by the FA and certain 'members' of Her Majesty's Press"*, probably don't come under the banner of the research we are now going to discuss. You see, these studies aren't subtle enough to describe their behaviour.

Anyway, let's begin.

Michael Hogg and Graham Vaughan note a dramatic reduction in anti-black attitudes in the United States since the 1930s. Much the same has occurred with respect to ethnic minorities in Britain and Western Europe. Hogg and Vaughn ask: should we conclude that racial prejudice has disappeared in Western industrial nations? They go on to say that because explicit and blatant racism (derogatory stereotypes, name-calling, abuse, persecution, assault and discrimination) is illegal and thus socially censured, it is now more difficult to find; therefore, most people in most contexts do not behave in this way.[1]

They move onto point out that racism may not only have gone 'underground'; it may actually have changed its form. This idea lies at the heart of a number of theories of 'new' or 'modern' racism. People may still be racist at heart, but in a different way – they may represent and express racism differently, perhaps more subtly.[2] Let's now have a look at one of these theories which probably played a part in the reaction of some Reds against Patrice Evra.

DOVIDIO AND GAERTNER put forward a theory called *Aversive Racism*. Aversive racism is a form of bias that is not overtly expressed but may reflect the attitudes of a substantial portion of people in societies that have strong egalitarian traditions and norms. Much of the research on aversive racism has focused on the orientation of Whites toward Blacks in the United States, but similar attitudes have been found among members of dominant groups in other countries with strong contemporary egalitarian values but discriminatory histories or policies. I think we can safely place Britain here.

Dovidio and Gaertner highlight in contrast to the traditional form of racism, which is expressed openly and directly, aversive racism operates in subtle and indirect ways. For example, the negative feelings that aversive racists have toward Blacks do not manifest themselves in open hostility or hatred. Instead, aversive racists' reactions may involve discomfort, anxiety, and/or fear. That is, they find Blacks "aversive," while at the same time rejecting any suggestion that they might be prejudiced.[3]

A critical aspect of the aversive racism framework is the conflict between aversive racists' denial of personal prejudice and underlying unconscious negative feelings toward and beliefs about particular minority groups. Because aversive racists consciously recognise and endorse egalitarian values and because they truly aspire to be unprejudiced, they will *not* act inappropriately in situations with strong social norms when discrimination would be obvious to others and to themselves.

Specifically, studies have shown that when they are presented with a situation in which the normatively appropriate response is clear, in which right and wrong are clearly defined, aversive racists will not discriminate against Blacks. In these contexts, aversive racists will be especially motivated to avoid feelings, beliefs, and behaviours that could be associated with racist intent. Wrongdoing of this type would directly threaten their image of themselves as non-prejudiced.[4]

Aversive racists still possess unconscious negative feelings and beliefs, however, which will eventually be expressed in subtle, indirect, and rationalizable ways. For instance, discrimination will occur in situations in which the normative structure is weak, the guidelines for appropriate behaviours are vague, or the basis for social judgment is ambiguous.

In addition, discrimination will occur when an aversive racist can justify or rationalise a negative response on the basis of some factor other than race. Studies show that under these circumstances, White aversive racists may engage in behaviours that ultimately harm Blacks, but in ways that allow the racists to maintain their self-image as unprejudiced and that insulate them from recognising that their behaviour is not colour-blind.[5]

In terms of combating aversive racism, traditional prejudice-reduction techniques have been concerned with changing conscious attitudes—old-fashioned racism—and obvious expressions of bias. Attempts to reduce this direct, traditional form of racial prejudice have typically involved educational strategies to enhance knowledge and appreciation of other groups (e.g., multicultural education programs), emphasise norms that prejudice is wrong, and involve direct (e.g., mass media appeals) or indirect (dissonance reduction) attitude change techniques. However, because aversive racism is pervasive, subtle, and complex, the traditional techniques for eliminating bias that focus on the immorality of prejudice and illegality of discrimination are not effective for combating it. Aversive racists recognise that prejudice is bad, but they may not recognise that *they* are prejudiced.[6]

Nevertheless, aversive racism can be addressed with techniques aimed at its roots at both the individual and collective levels. At the individual level, strategies to combat aversive racism can be directed at unconscious attitudes. For example, extensive training to create new, counter stereotypical associations with social categories (e.g., Blacks) can inhibit the unconscious activation of stereotypes, an element of aversive racists' negative attitudes. In addition, aversive racists' conscious attitudes, which are already favourable, can be instrumental in motivating change. Allowing aversive racists to become aware, in a non-threatening way, of their unconscious negative attitudes, feelings, and beliefs can stimulate self-regulatory processes. Such processes not only elicit immediate deliberative responses reaffirming conscious unprejudiced orientations (such as increased support for policies that benefit minority groups), but also produce, with sufficient time and experience, reductions in implicit negative beliefs and attitudes.[7]

On Dovidio and Gaertner's points of:

- wrongdoing of this type would directly threaten their image of themselves as non- prejudiced.
- aversive racist can justify or rationalise a negative response on the basis of some factor other than race.
- white aversive racists may engage in behaviours that ultimately harm Blacks, but in ways that allow the racists to maintain their self-image as unprejudiced and that insulate them from recognising that their behaviour is not colour-blind.

These 3 themes chime with me in relation to the podcasts we came across. One could contend these broadcasts were dripping in modern racism.

SEVENTEEN
NO SURRENDER TO PATRICE EVRA

Liverpool FC came into existence in 1892. What many people don't realise is that LFC wanted to be called Everton Athletic but were not allowed to by the English FA. This was due to the fact Everton FC already existed.

You see, LFC was formed because of a boardroom split within EFC. Now you are probably wondering "And"? Well, stay with me because I will now explain a third theory why LFC as a club and massive sections of their supporter base made Patrice Evra's life a living hell and it goes back to the very foundations of the club in the north of the city. And I believe, it's within this third idea where we can place the vast majority of fans.

I THINK TODAY, most people in the UK are aware that Liverpool is a left-leaning city. Indeed, the idea that the Conservatives could be electorally successful in Liverpool is so implausible that following the city's 2012 mayoral election, *BBC Radio 5 Live* reported that the Conservative candidate was defeated by a rival dressed as a polar bear.[1] However, this is a relatively recent phenomenon. Historically, the city was in many respects a Tory town. The Conservative Party was the dominant political force from the mid-eighteenth century and remained so until the middle of the 20th century.[2]

As proof that there has always been strong Conservative support in Liverpool, here are a few basic facts. At one time the Liverpool Working Men's Conservative Organisation was the country's strongest, and the Liverpool Conservatives agency was the largest in the country. The Working Men's Conservative Organisation founded in 1868, had twelve flourishing branches by 1872 with representation on all committees of the Constitutional Association. Its importance was such that Liverpool politics have to be seen through this lens.[3] In 1914, the Labour Party occupied only seven of a possible 140 seats on the city council, and it was only in 1955 that Labour achieved its first municipal majority in the city. Despite Labour's victory in the mid-1950s, the Conservatives averaged 49.8% of votes cast in local elections in that decade and 51.1% in the 1960s. Let me repeat that: in the swinging '60s whilst one Scouser was doing his bed love-in in Amsterdam, another 51.1% of Scousers voted Tory. And it was only in 1972 that the Conservatives lost control for the final time.[4]

So whilst in the late 19th and the early part of 20th centuries many working-class people around the country (and of course some in Liverpool too) were fighting for workers' rights and trying to form trade unions and laying the foundations for what would eventually become the Labour Party, many working-class people in our city voted Tory, Liberal and Irish Nationalist.

So why was this the case? Well, it was down to the city

being a port city and not a manufacturing town, and down to its geography, meaning there was huge immigration of Irish workers. And as Dunleavy points out, although anti-Irishness was a prominent feature of life in British society throughout the 19th and much of the 20th century, it was exhibited in extraordinary dimensions in Liverpool as it moulded the popular Conservatism and Labour Party to a degree unseen anywhere else in England.[5]

In truth, due to religion, Liverpool was politically backward in comparison with other English cities and it is a legacy the city is still struggling with even today. Let's now put this historical background within the connection of Liverpool's two main football clubs.

YOU SEE, whilst the split within the Everton board was taking place the biggest issue of the day in north Liverpool was that of Home Rule, the movement that campaigned for an independent Ireland, a subject that would also emphasise the differing nature of Liverpool's two major football clubs. In terms of the timeline, LFC was formed in March 1892 and the general election took place in July 1892, and Home Rule played a massive part in the campaign. As Jeffery explains, those against Home Rule tended to vote for the Conservatives, whilst those in favour voted for the Irish Nationalist Party (in its various guises),[6] and the Liberal Party too.

One clarion for the 1892 General Election was sounded by the new Conservative candidate for Liverpool, Houston: the granting of Home Rule, he said, "would mean civil war in Ireland".[7] The Liverpool Orangemen, "that very important and powerful body", in Houston's opinion, would not "stand quietly by and see their kinsmen and the loyalists of Ulster massacred and slaughtered".[8]

Along with politicians, and here is the key to the concept, there were many public statements made by prominent club representatives of both Everton and Liverpool FC concerning the issues of religion, ethnicity and the all-pervasive matter of Irish Home Rule—statements that would have driven home their differences for any interested outside audience. For example, Irish Everton director Dr William Whitford—described in the local press as 'an ardent Home-Ruler'—made an impassioned speech during the municipal election campaign of 1892 against the blocking of Irish Home Rule by Ulster unionists. He announced:

"Ulstermen do not desire to govern Ireland according to the wishes of the people of Ireland, but according to the narrow prejudices of the so-called 'loyal minority'."[9]

Another Everton director, Liberal councillor Alfred Gates (a name which was "as a red rag to a furious bull" to the Conservative-Unionist Party, according to the *Liverpool Daily Post*), was, according to Kennedy, a "strenuous advocate of Home Rule" and keen to show that "the Orange Tory Party were losing ground in Liverpool". Speaking to a Liberal-Nationalist audience, Gates suggested that "if Liberalism had a little of the enthusiasm and spirit of the Irish it would be in a better position today."[10]

Dr James Clement Baxter, a director, later chairman [of Everton], and a prominent Liberal Catholic who financed much of the building of Goodison Park, was the most identifiable link between Everton and Irish Catholicism. An example of this is he brought with him the thousands of Irish Catholic families from the Scotland Road area who duly became Everton supporters.[11]

In contrast to Liverpool FC's Protestant constituents, "frequent press reports of directors James Clement Baxter and Alfred Wade attending Irish Nationalist League meetings would have underlined for the public a sense of the general sectarian tone of the men inhabiting the Everton boardroom." Though George Mahon was a "staunch Methodist and organist at St Domingo parish church", he was also an advocate of Irish home-rule. Although born in Liverpool, he was brought up and educated in Ireland.[12]

THE POLITICAL RHETORIC of EFC officials was the polar opposite of their counterparts across the park. As Kennedy highlights from figures amongst the Liverpool FC hierarchy, on the other hand, there was an equally strident and public outpouring of feeling toward the Protestant-Unionist cause. Founder and chairman of Liverpool FC, John Houlding, quite obviously found it difficult to contain his religious leanings as a Conservative-Unionist and an Orangeman whilst carrying out his duties as a guardian at the West Derby Poor Law Union.

Guardians were elected to their positions by rate payers and were responsible for the administration of poor relief in their area—in this instance, a huge swathe of land that encompassed the whole of the north end districts of Liverpool and beyond to neighbouring towns, such as Bootle, Seaforth, Waterloo and Crosby, making it the biggest Poor Law Union in the country.[13] As Kennedy suggests, Houlding held huge power, and he pointedly refused to grant Catholic priests any payment for ministering to Catholic inmates of workhouses within his jurisdiction, whilst allowing such payment to Church of England and

Nonconformist ministers. In a letter published in the *Liverpool Courier*, Houlding set out his opposition to a motion put before the Poor Law Union to also allow payment to Catholic priests as an act of justice and common fairness:

"I defy any member of the Board or any judge in the land to show me an Act of Parliament which expressly stated that they should pay Roman Catholics for services performed in workhouses. If English Unions did appoint a Roman Catholic priest it is only done by a clear evasion of the law, and often perhaps for the sake of quietness."[14]

Another director, Edwin Berry, the successor to John Houlding as club chairman, made plain his opposition to the re-emergence of an influential Roman Catholic Church in British society. Addressing an audience of the National Protestant Union in 1898, an Evangelical Anglican body committed to helping "sound Protestant" candidates at elections, Berry offered his support to "the repression of lawlessness and Romanising influence", declaring himself to be a "loyal Churchman with every desire to further the principles of the Church of England in accordance with the Reformation".[15]

When the split came within Everton, the substantial Conservative presence at Liverpool is especially noteworthy, with eleven of the twenty-one directors and administrators of the club between 1892 and 1902 actively involved in Conservative politics.[16] The level and nature of the Liverpool hierarchy's involvement in Conservative politics is of particular interest. Six directors—Benjamin E. Bailey, Edwin Berry, John Houlding, William Houlding, Simon Jude and John McKenna—were members of the Constitutional Association, the ruling body of Liverpool Conservatism. The Constitutional Association exercised complete control over district Conservative associations in Liverpool, and affiliated societies and organisations such as the Orange Lodge.[17]

This Orange Lodge bit is key to understanding the fundamental attitude of the club today. For me Dalglish's attitude throughout the episode was symbolic of this, as was the language used by the likes of Andy Heaton: "Then you have the biggest hypocrite of them all, Mr Ferguson, whose anger on the subject turned his nose a purpler shade of puce". The nastiness of Dalglish and Heaton showed towards Evra seeps into them through those origins.

Emphasising LFC's strong ties with Protestantism, modern-day Orange Lodge Grand Master Ron Bather says:

"Primarily Liverpool was a very Protestant football club. The initial teams [...] when it was formed, you had to be a Protestant to be a player. Virtually all the initial team that played for Liverpool were all Scottish Presbyterian religion. If you go back to the 1920s and 30s Liverpool was considered the Protestant team and Everton the Catholic."[18]

In addition to Bather, Lodge Master and Liverpool fan, Dave Hughes, suggests that: "The Orange connection between the Orange Institution and Liverpool Football Club was very, very firm at one time."[19]

With the exception of Dalglish and Heaton the above is the theory. In the next chapter allow me to give you some evidence to support this claim that does not only involve the Evra-Suarez case.

EIGHTEEN

AN ACCIDENT

On 29 May 1985 at the European Cup Final, thirty-nine, mainly Italian Juventus fans, lost their lives in a violence-induced crush on the crumbling terraces of the Heysel Stadium in Brussels. There were many aspects to the tragedy, however, the main cause was down to LFC fans ripping down a dividing fence and creating panic amongst the opposition supporters. As a result, all English clubs were banned indefinitely from European competitions. LFC were given an additional 3-year ban which would come into play once other English clubs had been readmitted.

On 24 June 1985, UEFA wrote to Liverpool informing them of their punishment. The letter read:

"The supporters of Liverpool FC have shown an undisciplined, aggressive and extremely violent conduct towards spectators, who in their great majority were of Italian origin and also towards the security forces. Furthermore, they had demolished the fence separating the two sectors. In particular, they threw missiles (bottles etc.) and fired rockets against spectators in the other sector. Approximately one hour before the official kick-off of the match, they launched repeated attacks against the spectators concerned, causing ultimately to the death of 38 people [the thirty-ninth victim, Luigi Pidone, who had been in a coma, died from head injuries on 14 August] and injuries to 300 to 400 spectators, some remaining in a critical state."[1]

On 8 August, Liverpool appealed the ban. The club spoke about its fans' record in its four previous European Cup Finals. It stated: "No serious problems before, during or after the matches were experienced."[2] This is factually untrue. There were huge problems in Paris in 1981. Fans wrecked hotels and two Frenchmen were slashed, one across the throat with a Stanley Knife.

They then moved on to their punishment. They claimed that although there was abundant evidence of gross negligence on the part of the organising authorities, Liverpool had received the most severe punishment. They believed the punishment was unfair because it imposed a sanction which had no time limit. For them, this meant it destroyed incentive and motivation. They believed it could lead to the demise of Liverpool as a major European sporting institution, whilst its competitive future remained uncertain.

The club thought their suspension should be reduced for five main reasons. First, they claimed it was "Inappropriate". Under this heading Liverpool said that the deaths were not a direct cause of the violence, but a consequence of the inadequate stadium, poor policing, and improper ticket sales. Next was: "Too Severe". Here, the club mentioned that an indefinite ban could make recruitment of new players more difficult.

Third was "Unjust". They pointed out that the "Exemplary Punishment" was in contrary to all principals of natural justice. Next was "Uneven". The club suggested it could be fairly said that the behaviour of the Italians throughout was far more violent than the action of Liverpool followers, which lasted for a very short time. They ended with "Appearance of Justice". Here, they highlighted the role of UEFA. They said UEFA themselves should bear responsibility for their choice of stadium and failure to supervise ticket and segregation arrangements. They suggested that UEFA should not be seen to be imposing excessive punishments on others, which might be thought to draw attention away from their own involvement.

Liverpool concluded that they could not be considered either morally or in law at fault for this 'accident'. They also requested that their suspension should end when English clubs were once again considered fit to be admitted back to European competition.[3] The document LFC sent to UEFA was sixty pages long. As we can see from the evidence above you could hardly call it tactful. In fact, it is fair comment to say the document is shameful given fans lost their lives attending a football match.

IN TERMS OF SUAREZ-EVRA, the treatment of their ex-player, Howard Gayle, who we have mentioned previously, by the club reinforces the point I'm making. Gayle noted that he constantly gets asked why he doesn't work at Liverpool, why he doesn't appear on LFC TV, and why he doesn't work at the lounges on matchdays?[4] Well, here's possibly why.

Gayle explained that a few weeks after the incident he was working in a lounge at Anfield. During a Q&A session a fan asked him, "What do you think?"' Gayle told the gathering that Suarez was "[...] absolutely bang out of order." The club were not happy with their ex-player. They believed Gayle should have dodged the question or at least toned down his answer. When he first heard about the incident, he had supported the club's stance, however when he heard the full story his viewpoint altered. Gayle said:

"[...] when he kept on repeating it and repeating it then that comes a case of, he's using a term which is a racist term against a black player. And although it's against a Manchester United player, it doesn't matter to me. I'm a staunch Liverpool fan, but I'm black before I'm a Liverpool fan."

Gayle went on:

"And I have children and friends who I'm responsible for and people see me as a role model who constantly speaks out for them and constantly has the thoughts of them and their feelings in my heart. And when I heard that it gutted me, and it gutted a lot of people. So obviously, I didn't get any more work after that."[5]

Putting these incidents together it makes it clear to me there is a connection with how LFC responded to Evra and Heysel. Fanatical Orangemen founded the club and that dedication to a cause has never left them. Roots will always be roots and LFC's are Orange. Therefore, along with out-and-out racism, intergroup behaviour, and modern racism, the quality of not being able to compromise is one of the plausible reasons why the club and many of its fans returned to the 1890s during the Suarez episode. It is simply "No Surrender".

NINETEEN
FINAL THOUGHTS

Patrice Evra recently commented that he couldn't call Luis Suarez a racist. This was because he didn't know him closely enough, however, he believed that on that day, Suarez used some racist words. He added he has forgiven the Uruguayan.[1] Luis Suarez said he still felt aggrieved over being found guilty of racism. When asked if he regretted his past behaviour, which included a few high-profile biting incidents, he proclaimed:

"When I say I'm sorry it's because I regret something. Being sorry implies regret. But they have also sometimes judged me on things that aren't true, such as the racism thing."

He went on: "I was accused without evidence and that's what grieved me the most. The others were actions when it was me who did wrong. I accepted that and begged forgiveness, but the racism thing, when I was accused without evidence, that did upset me."[2]

A few months after the incident Kenny Dalglish admitted he should have handled the episode in a better way. He stated:

"It would be done completely differently if it ever happened again – and I hope it never does."

He continued:

"I wouldn't say publicly what I would do differently, but I know what I would do differently. I would address that. If I have done something wrong, I am not shy in saying I have done something wrong. If I can do something better, I will try and do it better. Everybody can look at themselves, whether they are good, bad, or indifferent and say: 'I could do things much better.' That is what I will try to do. I would certainly hope not to do things any worse."[3]

At the end of the 2011-12 season, Dalglish was fired. Alex Ferguson believes Dalglish was sacked in part because of his mishandling of the row. Ferguson observed:

"I wasn't surprised at Kenny leaving. I think John Henry [the Liverpool owner] has obviously looked at the Suarez incident and felt it wasn't handled in the right way. I think that must have been part of it. It certainly wasn't a nice thing to happen, you know."[4]

In relation to Dalglish, Evra asserted he hated Dalglish for his role in events and that it was karma when the Scot lost his job.[5]

In February 2018, Patrice Evra made his West Ham debut. Unfortunately for him, it was at Anfield. You would have thought by now, given the significance of what had happened, Reds would have acted with human decency towards the Frenchman. No chance unfortunately. Ahead of kick-off the left-back's name was booed when the teams were read out. Evra was heavily barracked and branded a liar by Liverpool supporters. The defender's every touch was booed. And following a minor spat during a first-half stoppage in play he came in for further stick.[6] The Kop sang:

"One lying b*****d." They also sang Suarez's name.⁷

IF YOU WERE BORN and grew up in Britain there should be only one conclusion you can draw in relation to the whole episode. And that deduction is the correct verdict was reached when Luis Suarez was found guilty of racially abusing Patrice Evra. However, we know lots of British born Reds followed Suarez and their club down a path which goes against how a modern civilised country should conduct itself. One of the most nauseating justifications I saw for defending Suarez was this:

"The city of Liverpool has always correctly welcomed a righteous siege, and the last stand of the Suarez citadel feels like a fort worthy of defending."⁸

You won't be surprised to know that it came from the *Anfield Wrap*. It's hideous on many levels. First, it totally dismisses any black person in the city. Second, they aren't speaking for me, and I would imagine any other fair-minded person in the city. It's stomach-turning that they are cynically dragging an entire city into a debate when the circumstances revolved around their management and sections of a football club's fanbase (many of whom aren't even from the city). Finally, for them to use the 1980s political situation in the city when the local council was politically at war with Margaret Thatcher's government is snake oilman stuff. Back then, the city was a mess and the unemployment rate was heart-breaking. For them to use this as a weapon to undermine the fight against racism is abhorrent.

Further to this you see many articles and *Twitter* comments by many of the people I've mentioned and my god these people really do hold the world to account. Additionally, they aren't shy at giving interviews to local, national and even international TV, radio and newspapers. Their views can often be in relation to non-football issues too. They regularly critique on how the UK should be a much more just and fairer society. However, wow betide anyone who bans their best player. As we have seen, their so-called principles they seem to cherish so dearly go out the window quicker than you can say:

"[...] if the word 'negreto' wasn't actually the word 'negreto' and began with a different letter."

And as we see now, we are in the realms of Groucho Marx and his principles.

As I said earlier, of the theories I have put forward, I think most Reds fall into the one connected to the Orange origins of the club, that spirit has never left them, and it manifests itself in an uncompromising attitude whatever the sensitivities of the circumstances. This means people can be on the sharp end of racist abuse. But for Reds like Neil Atkinson, John Gibbons, and Jay McKenna etc, that's a small price to pay when the alternative means losing your best player. For them, sounding barmy and in this case defending racism is a better scenario than any outsider tainting their club.

Madness.

BIBLIOGRAPHY

Books and Articles

Allen-Brade, Janice. "Black and white world." When Saturday Comes, (2012).

Dovidio, John D, & Samuel L. Gaertner, Encyclopaedia of Group Processes & Intergroup Relations Editors John M. Levine Michael A. Hogg. SAGE Publications, Inc. 2010. 48-51.

Hogg, Michael A, & Graham M. Vaughan. Social Psychology (Sixth Edition). London: Pearson Education Limited, 2011.

Jeffery, David. "The Strange Death of Tory Liverpool: Conservative electoral decline in Liverpool, 1945-1996." 2017.

Kennedy, David. Merseyside's Old Firm? The Sectarian Roots of Everton and Liverpool Football Clubs. Independently published, 2017.

Kennedy, David. "And then there were two: Everton and Liverpool football clubs, 1892–1902." Soccer & Society, 12:4, (2011): 523-537.

McCallam, Paul. Heysel Stadium Brussels: European Football's Darkest Hour. Paul McCallam Books. 2022.

Newby-Clark, I. Racial Ambivalence Theory Encyclopedia of Group Processes & Intergroup Relations Editors John M. Levine Michael A. Hogg. by SAGE Publications, Inc. 2010. 675-676.

Roberts, Keith. "The rise and fall of Liverpool sectarianism: An investigation into the decline of sectarian antagonism on Merseyside." PhD diss., University of Liverpool, 2015.

Tajfel, Henri, M. G. Billig, R.P. Bundy, & Claude Flament. "Social Categorisation and Intergroup Behaviour," *European Journal of Social Psychology* 1, no. 2 (1971): 149-178.

Tajfel, Henri. "Social Psychology of Intergroup Relations." *Annual review of Psychology* 33 (1982): 1-39.

Waller, P. J. Democracy & Sectarianism: A political and social history of Liverpool 1868–1939. Liverpool: Liverpool University Press, 1981.

Newspapers
Daily Mail
Daily Mirror
The Guardian
Liverpool Echo
The Metro

Reports
Goulding, Paul, Brian Jones, Denis Smith, FA and Luis Suarez. Reasons of the Regulatory Commission, 30 December 2011.

Others

Al Jazeera
The Anfield Wrap
BBC
The Daily Telegraph
The Diary of a CEO Clips
ESPN
Football Fans Podcast
Reuters
The Steven Howson Podcast
Sky Sports Football

NOTES

Introduction

1. Paul Goulding, Brian Jones, Denis Smith, "FA and Luis Suarez. Reasons of the Regulatory Commission," 30 December 2011.
2. Goulding, Jones, Smith, "FA and Luis Suarez."
3. Janice Allen-Brade, "Black and white world," When Saturday Comes, March 1 2012, https://www.wsc.co.uk/the-archive/black-and-white-world-2/
4. Allen-Brade, "Black and white world."

1. The Match

1. Andy Hunter "Squad sheets: Liverpool v Manchester United," The Guardian, October 14 2011, https://www.theguardian.com/football/2011/oct/14/squad-sheets-liverpool-manchester-united
2. Hunter, "Squad sheets."
3. Goulding, Jones, Smith, "FA and Luis Suarez."
4. Goulding, Jones, Smith, "FA and Luis Suarez."
5. Goulding, Jones, Smith, "FA and Luis Suarez."
6. Goulding, Jones, Smith, "FA and Luis Suarez."
7. Goulding, Jones, Smith, "FA and Luis Suarez."
8. Goulding, Jones, Smith, "FA and Luis Suarez."
9. Goulding, Jones, Smith, "FA and Luis Suarez."
10. Goulding, Jones, Smith, "FA and Luis Suarez."
11. ESPN staff, Suarez 'upset' by Evra race claims, October 16 2011, http://en.espn.co.uk/football/sport/story/116295.html

2. Charged

1. Goulding, Jones, Smith, "FA and Luis Suarez."
2. Goulding, Jones, Smith, "FA and Luis Suarez."
3. Sky Sports Premier League, "Patrice Evra discusses the racism incident with Luis Suarez in emotive interview/MNF," YouTube clip, https://www.youtube.com/watch?v=Zy--uBqVm3A
4. Goulding, Jones, Smith, "FA and Luis Suarez."

5. BBC Sport, "Luis Suarez charged with racially abusing Patrice Evra," November 17 2011, https://www.bbc.co.uk/sport/football/15764900
6. BBC Football, "Luis Suarez charged."
7. BBC Football, "Luis Suarez charged."
8. BBC Football, "Luis Suarez charged."

3. The Hearing

1. Goulding, Jones, Smith, "FA and Luis Suarez."
2. Goulding, Jones, Smith, "FA and Luis Suarez."
3. Goulding, Jones, Smith, "FA and Luis Suarez."
4. Goulding, Jones, Smith, "FA and Luis Suarez."
5. Goulding, Jones, Smith, "FA and Luis Suarez."
6. Goulding, Jones, Smith, "FA and Luis Suarez."

4. Decision

1. BBC Football, "Liverpool striker Luis Suarez handed eight-match FA ban," December 20 2011, http://www.bbc.com/sport/football/16186556
2. Daniel Taylor, "Liverpool furious as Luis Suarez banned in Patrice Evra racism row," The Guardian, December 20 2011, https://www.theguardian.com/football/2011/dec/20/liverpool-luis-suarez-patrice-evra
3. BBC Football, "Liverpool striker Luis Suarez handed eight-match FA ban."
4. BBC Football, "Liverpool striker Luis Suarez handed eight-match FA ban."
5. BBC Football, "Liverpool striker Luis Suarez handed eight-match FA ban."
6. BBC Football, "Liverpool striker Luis Suarez handed eight-match FA ban."
7. BBC Football, "Liverpool striker Luis Suarez handed eight-match FA ban."
8. Gregg Roughley, "Luis Suarez's racism ban: media reaction," The Guardian, December 21 2011, https://www.theguardian.com/football/2011/dec/21/luis-suarez-racism-ban-media-reaction
9. Roughley, "Luis Suarez's racism ban: media reaction."
10. Roughley, "Luis Suarez's racism ban: media reaction."
11. James Pearce, Liverpool FC: James' Pearce's verdict on the Luis Suarez ban, Liverpool Echo, December 21 2011, https://www.liverpoolecho.co.uk/sport/football/football-news/liverpool-fc-james-pearces-verdict-3358232

5. T-shirts

1. Jamie Carragher, "Liverpool made huge mistake with Luis Suarez T-shirts after Patrice Evra racism row," Sky Sports Football, October 22 2019, https://www.skysports.com/football/news/29327/11841683/jamie-carragher-liverpool-made-huge-mistake-with-luis-suarez-t-shirts-after-patrice-evra-racism-row
2. SimpleDragz, "Kenny Dalglish Post Match Interview Wigan V Liverpool," YouTube video, December 11 2011, https://www.youtube.com/watch?v=l4X7Hu7Jpoo
3. SimpleDragz, "Kenny Dalglish Post Match Interview Wigan V Liverpool."
4. Andy Hunter, "Liverpool shirts supporting Luis Suarez 'shameful', says Paul McGrath," The Guardian, December 22 2011, https://www.theguardian.com/football/2011/dec/22/liverpool-shirts-luis-suarez
5. The Steven Howson Podcast, "I'm a Liverpool fan but I'm black first." Howard Gayle on Evra/Suarez and Racism in the Game, https://www.youtube.com/watch?v=frqZpt8voCk
6. The Diary of a CEO Clips, "Has Patrice Evra Forgiven Luis Suarez"? https://www.youtube.com/watch?v=qxyj9zcYEEM
7. Carragher, "Liverpool made huge mistake with Luis Suarez T-shirts after Patrice Evra racism row."
8. Carragher, "Liverpool made huge mistake with Luis Suarez T-shirts after Patrice Evra racism row."
9. Carragher, "Liverpool made huge mistake with Luis Suarez T-shirts after Patrice Evra racism row."
10. Carragher, "Liverpool made huge mistake with Luis Suarez T-shirts after Patrice Evra racism row."
11. The Diary of a CEO Clips, "Has Patrice Evra Forgiven Luis Suarez"?
12. Hunter, "Liverpool shirts supporting Luis Suarez 'shameful', says Paul McGrath."
13. Hunter, "Liverpool shirts supporting Luis Suarez 'shameful', says Paul McGrath."
14. Hunter, "Liverpool shirts supporting Luis Suarez 'shameful', says Paul McGrath."
15. Allen-Brade, "Black and white world."
16. Sports Mail Reporter, "Dalglish insists Liverpool's T-shirt support for Suarez is 'the least he deserves'," Daily Mail, December 23 2011 https://www.dailymail.co.uk/sport/football/article-2077978/Kenny-Dalglish-defends-Liverpools-Luis-Suarez-T-shirts.html
17. Sports Mail Reporter, "Dalglish insists Liverpool's T-shirt support for Suarez is 'the least he deserves'."

6. "He Used Sudaca or Something."

1. Andy Heaton, "Suarez Reaction: The lads discuss the absolute fucking abomination of a case against Luis Suarez and the witch-hunt by the FA and certain 'members' of Her Majesty's Press," The Anfield Wrap, December 22 2011, https://www.theanfieldwrap.com/2011/12/the-anfield-wrap-suarez-reaction/
2. Goulding, Jones, Smith, "FA and Luis Suarez."
3. Goulding, Jones, Smith, "FA and Luis Suarez."
4. Neil Atkinson, "Suarez Reaction."
5. Atkinson, "Suarez Reaction."
6. Heaton, "Suarez Reaction."
7. Martin, "Suarez Reaction."

7. The Report

1. Goulding, Jones, Smith, "FA and Luis Suarez."
2. Goulding, Jones, Smith, "FA and Luis Suarez."
3. James Pearce, Liverpool FC weigh up Luis Suarez options in wake of independent regulatory commission report, Liverpool Echo, January 2 2012, https://www.liverpoolecho.co.uk/sport/football/football-news/liverpool-fc-weigh-up-luis-3354159
4. Pearce, "Liverpool FC weigh up Luis Suarez options in wake of independent regulatory commission report."
5. Pearce, "Liverpool FC weigh up Luis Suarez options in wake of independent regulatory commission report."

8. "There is no Smoking Gun in there."

1. Neil Atkinson, "Episode 23," The Anfield Wrap, January 2 2012, https://www.theanfieldwrap.com/2012/01/the-anfield-wrap-episode-twenty-three/
2. Girling, "Episode 23."
3. Gareth Roberts, "Episode 23."
4. Sky Sports Premier League, "Patrice Evra discusses the racism incident with Luis Suarez in emotive interview/MNF."
5. McKenna, "Episode 23."
6. McKenna, "Episode 23."
7. McKenna, "Episode 23."

9. There's More to the Report than Meets the Eye

1. Al Jazeera, "Liverpool will not appeal against Suarez ban," January 3 2012, https://www.aljazeera.com/sports/2012/1/3/liverpool-will-not-appeal-against-suarez-ban
2. Al Jazeera, "Liverpool will not appeal against Suarez ban."
3. Al Jazeera, "Liverpool will not appeal against Suarez ban."
4. Al Jazeera, "Liverpool will not appeal against Suarez ban."
5. Al Jazeera, "Liverpool will not appeal against Suarez ban."
6. Al Jazeera, "Liverpool will not appeal against Suarez ban."
7. Jack Prescott, "Liverpool players defend Luis Suarez," Sportsmole, Date Unknown,
   https://www.sportsmole.co.uk/football/liverpool/news/liverpool-players-defend-suarez_11152.html
8. Daniel Taylor "Transcript of Kenny Dalglish's press conference about Luis Suarez," The Guardian, January 4 2012,
   https://www.theguardian.com/football/2012/jan/04/kenny-dalglish-luis-suarez-transcript
9. Taylor, "Transcript of Kenny Dalglish's press conference about Luis Suarez."
10. Herman Ouseley, "Liverpool's hypocrisy undermines anti-racism and our young people," The Guardian, January 5 2012, https://www.theguardian.com/football/2012/jan/05/luis-suarez-liverpool
11. Ouseley, "Liverpool's hypocrisy undermines anti-racism and our young people."
12. Rob Gutmann, "Without Prejudice- The Curious Case of the Racist Non-Racist," The Anfield Wrap, January 6 2012, https://www.theanfieldwrap.com/2012/01/without-prejudice-the-curious-case-of-the-racist-non-racist/
13. Gutmann, "Without Prejudice- The Curious Case of the Racist Non-Racist."

10. "People Might Not Realise They Are Racist."

1. Mike Girling, "Episode 24," The Anfield Wrap, January 9 2012, https://www.theanfieldwrap.com/2012/01/the-anfield-wrap-episode-twenty-four/
2. Girling, "Episode 24."
3. Girling, "Episode 24."
4. Allen-Brade, "Black and white world."
5. Neil Atkinson, "FFP Racism in football special," Football Fans Podcast,

9 April 2019, https://twitter.com/FootballFansPod/status/1115526749524250625
6. Phil McNulty, "'Tormented' De Gea a great concern for Ferguson," BBC Sport, 28 January 2012, https://www.bbc.co.uk/blogs/philmcnulty/2012/01/sorrowful_and_tormented_de_gea.html
7. Gareth Roberts, "Who's Arsed?" The Anfield Wrap, January 29 2012, https://www.theanfieldwrap.com/2012/01/whos-arsed/
8. Metro Web Reporter, "Liverpool fan Phillip Gannon guilty of racially abusing Patrice Evra," The Metro, June 22 2012, https://metro.co.uk/2012/06/22/liverpool-fan-phillip-gannon-guilty-of-racially-abusing-manchester-uniteds-patrice-evra-477744/

11. "Bang out of Order."

1. Carragher, "Liverpool made huge mistake with Luis Suarez T-shirts after Patrice Evra racism row."
2. Andy Hunter, "Why didn't Liverpool appeal over Luis Suarez ban, asks Alex Ferguson," The Guardian, February 10 2012, https://www.theguardian.com/football/2012/feb/10/liverpool-luis-suarez-sir-alex-ferguson
3. Hunter, "Why didn't Liverpool appeal over Luis Suárez ban, asks Alex Ferguson."
4. Hunter, "Why didn't Liverpool appeal over Luis Suárez ban, asks Alex Ferguson."
5. Daniel Taylor, "Liverpool's Kenny Dalglish plays dumb to leave his dignity in tatters," The Guardian, February 11 2012, https://www.theguardian.com/football/blog/2012/feb/11/liverpool-kenny-dalglish-luis-suarez
6. YouGotTrolled123, "Manchester United V Liverpool FC Patrice Evra / Luis Suarez managers opinion of incident," YouTube video, https://www.youtube.com/watch?v=oHcGcJge2X4
7. Carragher, "Liverpool made huge mistake with Luis Suarez T-shirts after Patrice Evra racism row."
8. The Diary of a CEO Clips, "Has Patrice Evra Forgiven Luis Suarez"?
9. YouGotTrolled123, "Manchester United V Liverpool FC Patrice Evra / Luis Suarez managers opinion of incident."
10. Martin Sheenan, "Dalglish interview post-match," YouTube video, https://www.youtube.com/watch?v=MCXMQUscQRU
11. Sheenan, "Dalglish interview post-match."
12. BBC Football, "Players and pundits react to handshake row," BBC, February 11 2012, https://www.bbc.co.uk/sport/football/17000355
13. BBC Football, "Players and pundits react to handshake row."
14. Taylor, "Liverpool's Kenny Dalglish plays dumb to leave his dignity in tatters."

12. "Apologies Were Necessary."

1. Dan Roan, "Handshake: Suarez and Dalglish apologise after owners intervene," BBC, February 13 2012, http://beta.bbc.com/sport/0/football/17004667
2. Steve Slater & Keith Weir, "Liverpool owner and sponsor raised Suarez concerns," February 13 2012, https://www.reuters.com/article/soccer-liverpool-suarez-idINDEE81C0EE20120213
3. Roan, "Handshake: Suarez and Dalglish apologise after owners intervene."
4. Roan, "Handshake: Suarez and Dalglish apologise after owners intervene."
5. Roan, "Handshake: Suarez and Dalglish apologise after owners intervene."
6. Roan, "Handshake: Suarez and Dalglish apologise after owners intervene."
7. Roan, "Handshake: Suarez and Dalglish apologise after owners intervene."

13. "The Barbarians are at our Gates."

1. Andy Heaton, "You have the right to be offended-when it suits," The Anfield Wrap, 12 February 2012, https://www.theanfieldwrap.com/2012/02/you-have-the-right-to-be-offended---when-it-suits/
2. Heaton, "You have the right to be offended-when it suits."
3. Heaton, "You have the right to be offended-when it suits."
4. Rob Gutmann, "Us and Them– Time to pull up the drawbridge," The Anfield Wrap, February 14 2012, https://www.theanfieldwrap.com/2012/02/us-and-them-time-to-pull-up-the-drawbridge/
5. Allen-Brade, "Black and white world."
6. Allen-Brade, "Black and white world."

14. United Against Fascism

1. BBC News, "Liverpool FC accused of inciting racism by community groups," February 20 2012, https://www.bbc.co.uk/news/uk-england-merseyside-17101933
2. Andy Hunter, "Liverpool and Luis Suarez 'critically undermined' anti-racism efforts," The Guardian, February 20 2012, https://www.theguardian.com/football/2012/feb/20/liverpool-luis-suarez-anti-racism

3. Hunter, "Liverpool and Luis Suarez 'critically undermined' anti-racism efforts."
4. Hunter, "Liverpool and Luis Suarez 'critically undermined' anti-racism efforts."
5. Gloria Hyatt, "Liverpool Football Club must engage with the anti-racism cause," The Guardian, February 24 2012 https://www.theguardian.com/commentisfree/2012/feb/24/liverpool-football-club-anti-racism
6. Hyatt, "Liverpool Football Club must engage with the anti-racism cause."
7. Hyatt, "Liverpool Football Club must engage with the anti-racism cause."
8. Hyatt, "Liverpool Football Club must engage with the anti-racism cause."
9. The Diary of a CEO Clips, "Has Patrice Evra Forgiven Luis Suarez"?

15. Food Fights

1. Henri Tajfel, "Social Psychology of Intergroup Relations," *Annual Review of Psychology* 33 (1982).
2. Tajfel, "Intergroup Relations."
3. Michael A. Hogg & Graham M. Vaughan. Social Psychology (Sixth Edition). (London: Pearson Education Limited, 2011).
4. David Shariatmadari, "A real-life Lord of the Flies: The troubling legacy of the Robbers Cave experiment," The Guardian, April 16 2018, https://www.theguardian.com/science/2018/apr/16/a-real-life-lord-of-the-flies-the-troubling-legacy-of-the-robbers-cave-experiment.
5. Hogg and Vaughan, *Social Psychology*.
6. Henri Tajfel et al., "Social Categorisation and Intergroup Behaviour," *European Journal of Social Psychology* 1, no. 2 (1971).
7. Tajfel et al., "Social Categorisation."
8. Tajfel, "Intergroup Relations."
9. Hogg and Vaughan, *Social Psychology*.

16. Modern Racism

1. Hogg and Vaughan, *Social Psychology*.
2. Hogg and Vaughan, *Social Psychology*.
3. John F. Dovidio and Samuel L. Gaertner. Aversive Racism. Encyclopaedia of Group Processes & Intergroup Relations Editors John M. Levine Michael A. Hogg. 2010 by Sage Publications, Inc, 48-51
4. Dovidio and Gaertner, Aversive Racism.
5. Dovidio and Gaertner, Aversive Racism.

6. Dovidio and Gaertner, Aversive Racism.
7. Dovidio and Gaertner, Aversive Racism.

17. No Surrender to Patrice Evra

1. David Jeffery, "The Strange Death of Tory Liverpool: Conservative Electoral Decline in Liverpool, 1945-1996," *British Politics* 12 (2017).
2. Jeffery, "The Strange Death of Tory Liverpool."
3. P.J. Waller, *Democracy & Sectarianism: A political and social history of Liverpool 1868-1939* (Liverpool: Liverpool University Press, 1981).
4. Jeffery, "The Strange Death of Tory Liverpool."
5. Cameron Dunleavy, "How did the Development of Religious Sectarianism and Irish Nationalism Shape Liverpool's Political Environment from 1836 to 1939?".
6. David Jeffery. The Strange Death of Tory Liverpool: Conservative electoral decline in Liverpool, 1945-1996." British Politics 12 (2017): 386–407.
7. Waller, P. J. Democracy & Sectarianism: A political and social history of Liverpool 1868–1939. Liverpool: Liverpool University Press, 1981.
8. Waller, *Democracy & Sectarianism*.
9. David Kennedy, Merseyside's Old Firm? The Sectarian Roots of Everton and Liverpool Football Clubs. Independently published, 2017.
10. Kennedy, *Merseyside's Old Firm?*
11. Keith Roberts, The rise and fall of Liverpool sectarianism: An investigation into the decline of sectarian antagonism on Merseyside." PhD diss., University of Liverpool, 2015.
12. Roberts, *The rise and fall of Liverpool sectarianism*.
13. Kennedy, *Merseyside's Old Firm?*
14. Kennedy, *Merseyside's Old Firm?*
15. Kennedy, *Merseyside's Old Firm?*
16. Kennedy, *Merseyside's Old Firm?*
17. Kennedy, David. "And then there were two: Everton and Liverpool football clubs, 1892–1902." *Soccer & Society*, 12:4, (2011): 523-537.
18. Roberts, *The rise and fall of Liverpool sectarianism*.
19. Roberts, *The rise and fall of Liverpool sectarianism*.

18. An Accident

1. M. Daphinoff, *Letter from UEFA to LFC*, June 24, 1985.
2. *Documents Annexed to Submissions to UEFA Appeal*, August 8, 1985.
3. *Documents Annexed to Submissions to UEFA Appeal*.
4. The Steven Howson Podcast, "I'm a Liverpool fan but I'm black first."

5. The Steven Howson Podcast, "I'm a Liverpool fan but I'm black first."

19. Final Thoughts

1. The Diary of a CEO Clips, "Has Patrice Evra Forgiven Luis Suarez"?
2. Dermot Corrigan, Luis Suarez: I accept my mistakes but Patrice Evra racism incident 'upset me', ESPN, October 14 2014, https://www.espn.co.uk/football/league-name/story/2086968/headline
3. Press Association, "Kenny Dalglish regrets his handling of Liverpool's Luis Suarez racism row," 14 April 2012, https://www.theguardian.com/football/2012/apr/14/kenny-dalglish-luis-suarez-liverpool
4. David McDonnel, "Suicidal defending: Dalglish's support for Suarez got him fired – Fergie," Daily Mirror, July 20 2012, https://www.mirror.co.uk/sport/football/news/kenny-dalglish-got-himself-sacked-by-liverpool-1149787
5. The Diary of a CEO Clips, "Has Patrice Evra Forgiven Luis Suarez"?
6. Mike Keegan, "Patrice Evra abused by Liverpool fans at Anfield over Luis Suarez racism dispute as chants of 'lying b******' sour excellent victory over West Ham," Mail on Sunday, February 24 2018, http://www.dailymail.co.uk/sport/football/article-5431069/Patrice-Evra-abused-Liverpool-fans-West-Ham-debut.html?ITO=1490
7. Keegan, "Patrice Evra abused by Liverpool fans at Anfield over Luis Suarez racism dispute as chants of 'lying b******' sour excellent victory over West Ham."
8. Rob Gutmann, "Suarez: Why we must stand by our man," The Anfield Wrap, December 29 2011, https://www.theanfieldwrap.com/2011/12/suarez-why-we-must-stand-by-our-man/

ABOUT THE AUTHOR

Paul McCallam is from Liverpool. He has a BSc in Psychology and a BA in History & Politics.

It would be great to hear from you.
    mccapaul17@gmail.com

It would be nice of you to leave a review.

ALSO BY PAUL MCCALLAM

Book 1

Heysel Stadium Brussels: European Football's Darkest Hour

Book 2

Heysel Stadium Brussels: European Football's Darkest Hour The Short Version Read

www.ingramcontent.com/pod-product-compliance
Lightning Source LLC
Chambersburg PA
CBHW030303100526
44590CB00012B/496